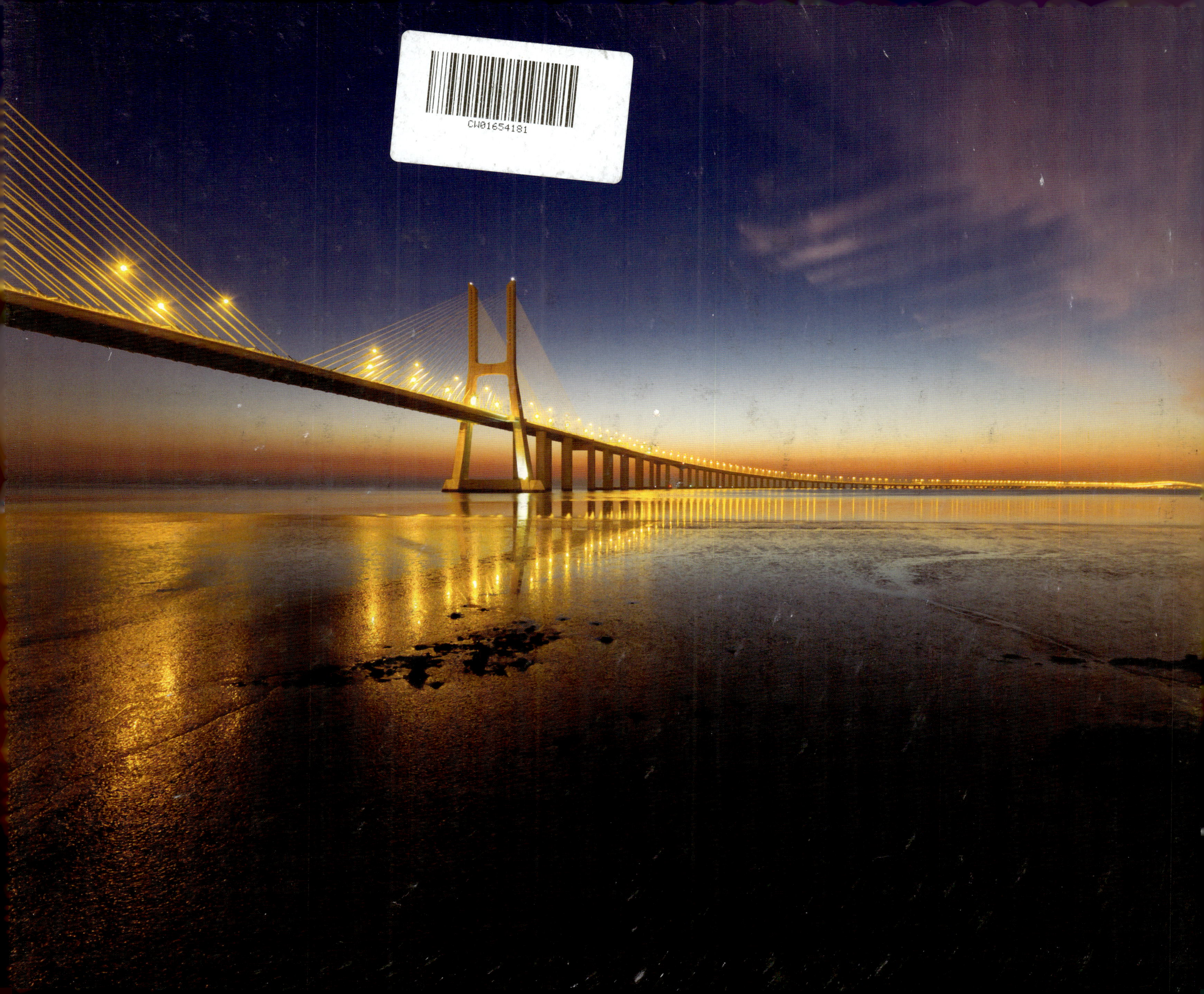

ISBN 978-0-9570402-0-5

Published by CBRE Limited

URBAN PHOTO-GRAPHER

OF THE YEAR

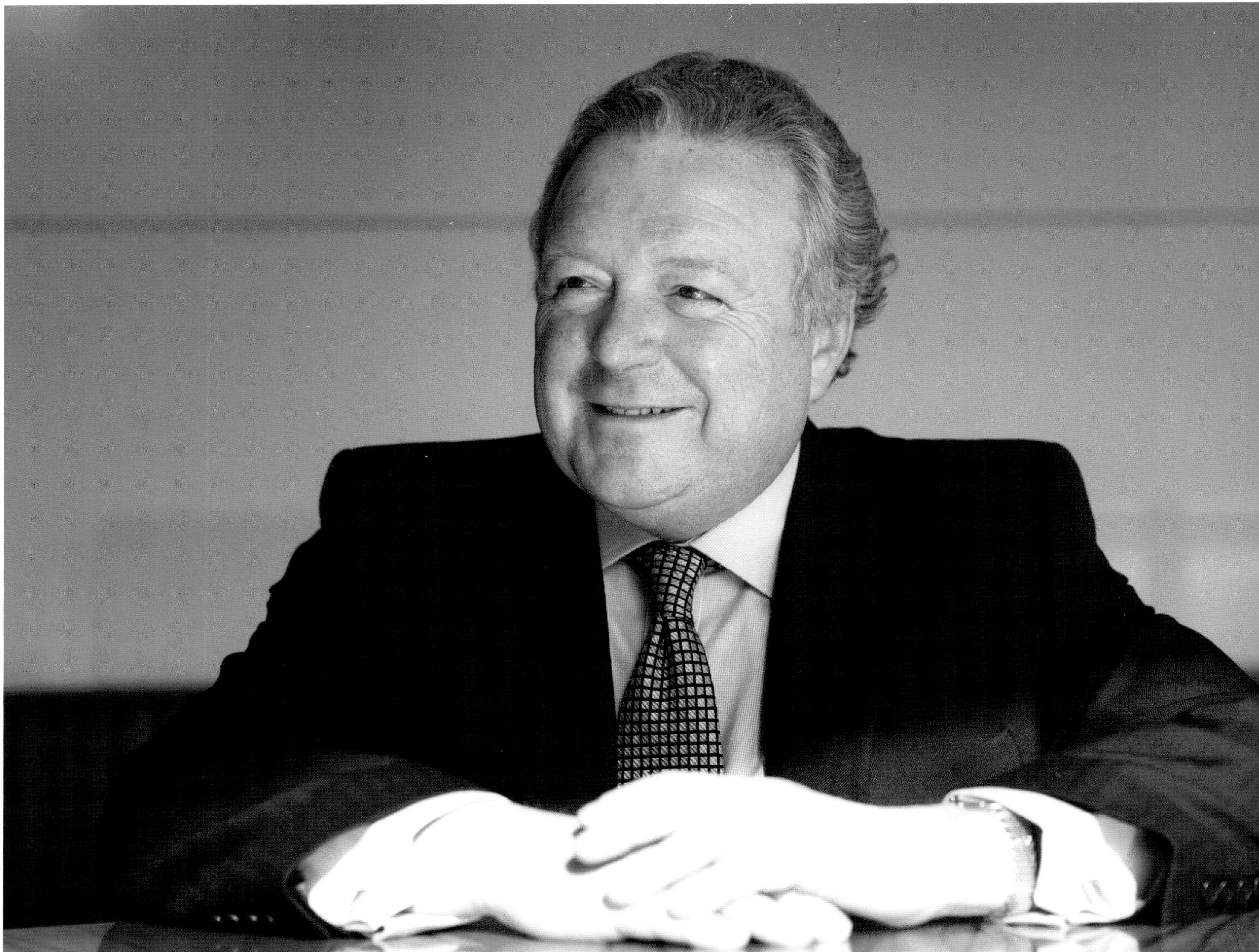

Foreword
Urban Photographer Of The Year

It is a great pleasure to introduce the Urban Photographer of the Year book celebrating the outstanding winners of the competition from across every corner of Europe, Middle East and Africa (EMEA). Over the years the competition has grown significantly and with it, I have been impressed and fascinated at the natural curiosity and challenge faced by our entrants to capture city life through the lens. It is this challenge that provides a natural reflection of our very own passion and understanding of the urban environment.

We have seen an extraordinary range of images from the tunnels beneath our feet, to the construction of a new bui ding, to the way we maintain our buildings and to the very way we travel to work every day.

Every urban landscape has its own nuances, demonstrated by the huge range of entries we received, and as a company with global reach and thousands of local specialists, understanding what makes different cities tick is how we deliver depth of knowledge to our clients.

I hope you enjoy the superb photographs that follow.

Mike Strong
CBRE Chairman, EMEA

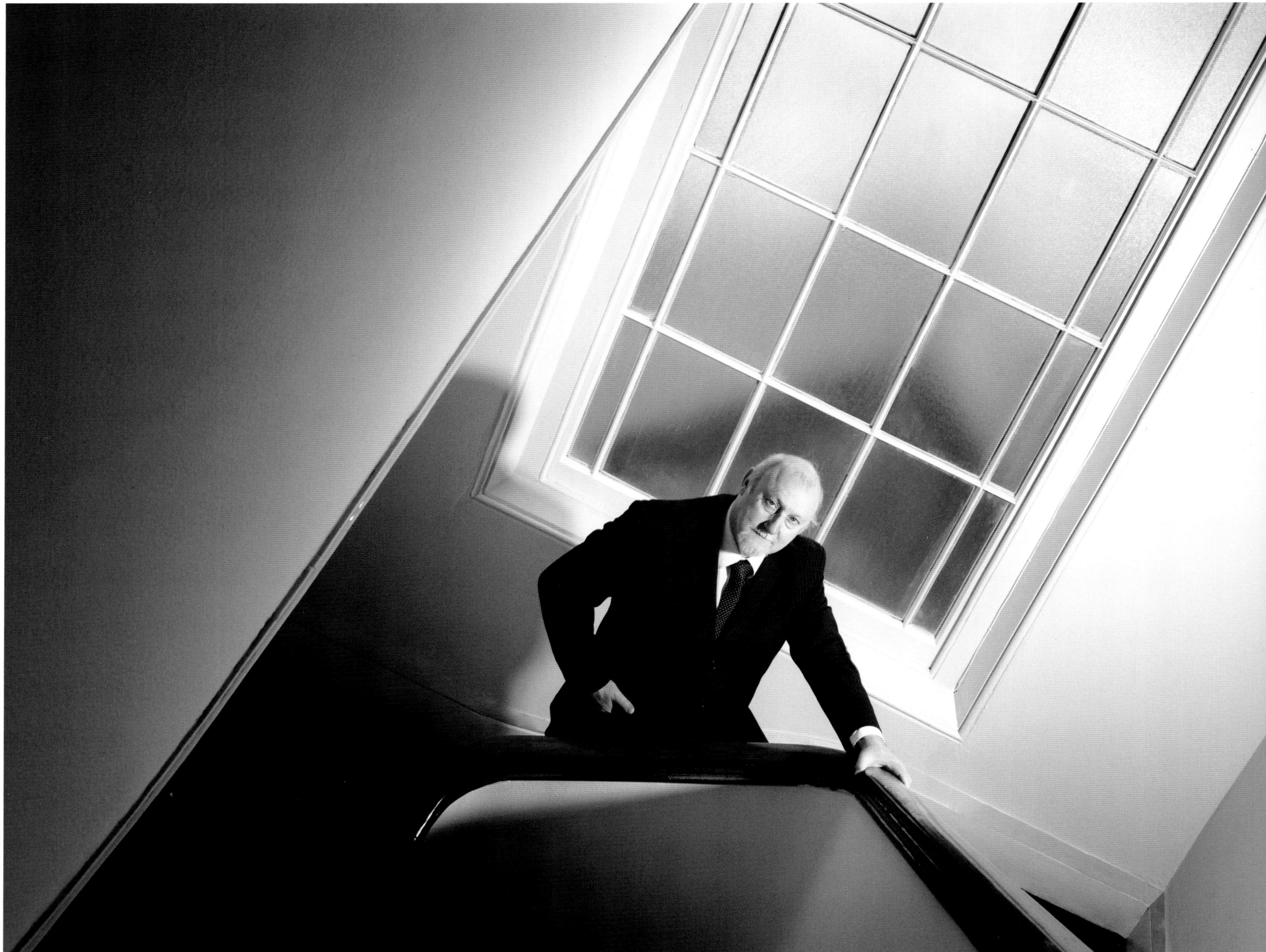

The Judges Panel
Urban Photographer of the Year

I was a fan of the idea of the competition from the moment I first heard about it but I did not expect it to create such a change in my understanding. Urban photography is a much neglected part of our social heritage. Seen by many as co-incidental - a by product of modern life, rather than a deliberate and creative activity. So when I was asked to chair the Panel of Judges for what was initially a UK based competition, I was allowed to witness the opening of a new and exciting door in photography. The natural affinity of CBRE to the subject made sense not just professionally but also geographically - they are everywhere!

However, nothing prepared me for the meteoric growth of the competition. Quickly expanding to encompass Europe, The Middle East and Africa, the competition now attracts more than 10,000 images from over 65 countries, from photographers from all walks of life. We have seen beautiful architectural photography, stunning in its geometric perfection; deeply insightful documentary photography; together with random acts of 'being in the right place at the right time' photography. We have seen lives played out across the spectrum of time and place and it has been humbling to observe.

I love the format with its ability to offer every kind of photographer the chance to participate and win. Every hour of the day comes alive from thousands of different perspectives and that is what, makes this one of the modern world's most important photographic references. In twenty years time, many of the sights, styles and objects photographed and submitted to the competition, will be obsolete. You will no longer see the makes of car, the style of clothing, the type of building. The competition becomes a marker in time.

But the most important thing I have learned from judging the competition is how amazingly similar we all are. The sum of the differences is miniscule compared to the similarities. At any given hour of the day we are all doing similar things - eating our breakfast, travelling to work, relaxing for lunch, travelling home in the dark. Over half the world's population now live in cities. These mundane elements are part of our every day lives and are no less important for their frequency.

Humans are creatures of habit, we all feel comfortable in our own routines and familiar ways. The glory of this competition is that it has shown me that rather than focus on the things that separate us and make us different, as so many media companies would like us to keep in mind – in fact, we have far more in common than we ever stop to consider - things that make us content and at peace; simple little things that it takes a photographer to notice.

In demonstrating these similarities I think that the CBRE Urban Photographer of the Year competition has genuinely contributed to the archive of our time on this planet.

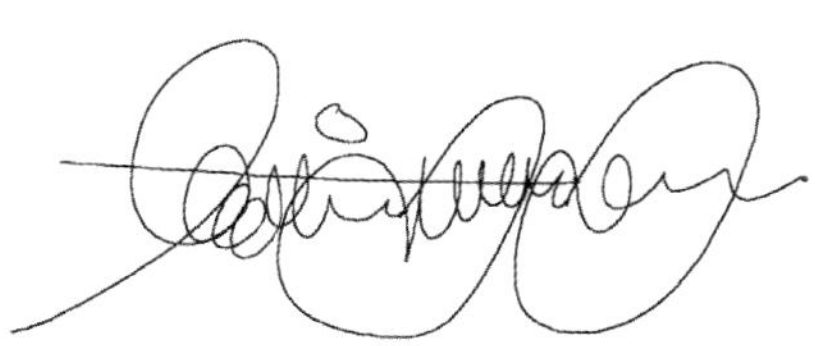

Martin C. Grahame Dunn
FMPA, FRSA, Hon. FMPA, QEP;
Chairman of Judges

The Brief
'Cities at Work'

The competition was designed to offer a clear brief - as advised by our advertising colleagues – keep it sharp and simple – Cities at Work. But we felt that the problem with photo competitions was that only one person wins and only one prize is ever discussed. So we redesigned and came up with our unique 'day in the life' structure. Thanks to our great sponsors we can offer amazing photographic prizes and still have a tight brief. It is the time of day that changes. This suits photographers as they observe changes in mood and light as well as the regular changes in the daily cycle of urban life. The light plays on the buildings and the people – it creates new opportunities and challenges every hour – and that is where the photographers come in.

Other Judges on the 2011 Panel
Urban Photographer of the Year

Marianne Lind
Freelance Photographer

Hussein Ali Aljassim
An Official in the Alhassa Photography Group

Ralf Pascual
CBRE Urban Photographer of the Year, 2009

Armen Dolukhanyan
Hourly winner in the CBRE Urban Photographer of the Year Award, 2009

Moray Maclennan
Worldwide CEO, M&C Saatchi

Derek Poulston
Managing Director, One Vision Imaging

2010
WINNERS

1st Place Winner, 2010

Name: Victor Melo, 46
Nationality: Portuguese
Status: Amateur
Photographer since: 1990
Favourite Camera of all Time: Canon EOS 5
Influences: Eduardo Gageiro, Sebastião Salgado, Henri Cartier-Bresson, Don McCullin

The Location: Tunis, Tunisia

The Story: This photograph was taken in Tunisia while exploring the labyrinthine souk, in the heart of the city of Tunis. Passing this craftsman working in the street, our eyes met and, without having to utter any words, I asked his permission to take a photograph. He agreed, quietly continued his work and I quickly measured the light, speed, frame and shot. The moment I saw this craftsman, calm and safe, doing his work, turning raw metal into art, in the middle of the train of people, noisy and frenetic, I thought this man is alone in the crowd. These days, we live in haste and forget to stop to look, and enjoy life as a rare piece of art.

The Exposure:
Camera: Canon EOS 400D
Lens: Tamron AF 18-270mm F/3.5-6.3 Di II VC @ 90mm
Settings: F5,6 @ 1/100 sec ISO 400
Post-production: Photoshop

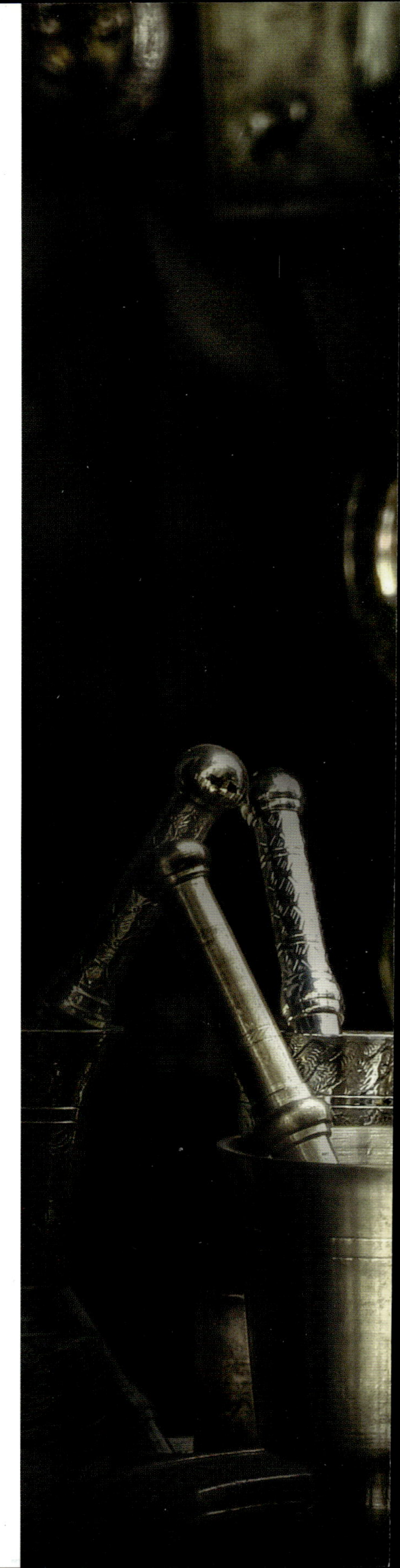

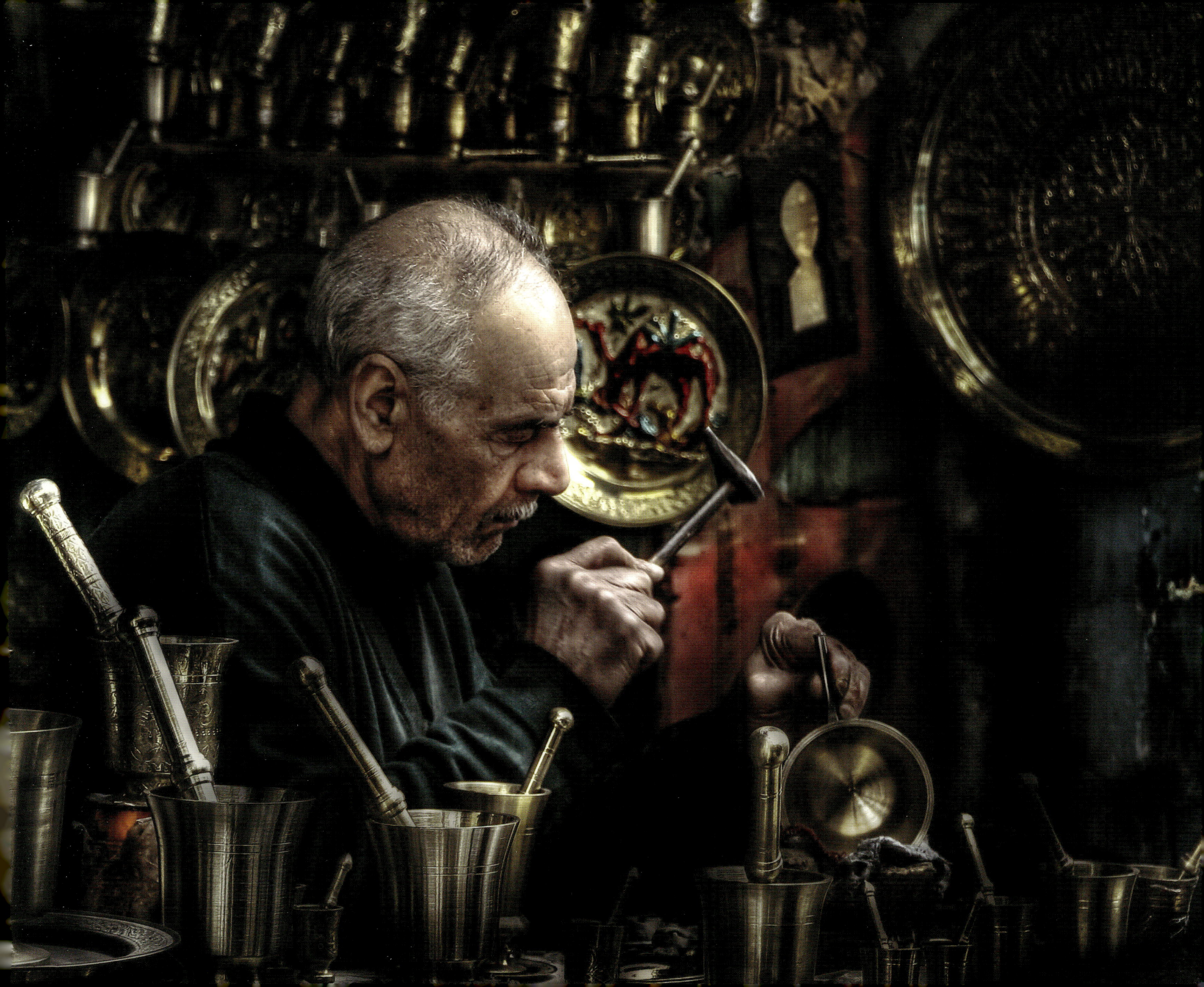

2nd Place Winner, 2010

Name: Tobias Weisserth, 33
Nationality: German
Status: Amateur
Photographer since: 1998
Favourite Camera of all Time: Minolta XD7
Influences: Henri Cartier-Bresson, Richard I'Anson

The Location: Hamburg, Germany

The Story: On my commute back home from work, I noticed everybody trying to get home as quickly as possible, potentially only deviating by running shopping errands and such. I was fascinated with how each individual in that anonymous mass of commuters is a space in itself. I wanted to capture this and started with the ultimate symbol of an urban individual in motion – the cyclist. Unlike everybody else, I delayed my commute home, on purpose, to capture other commuters. I wanted to show them disconnected from the world around, yet still preserve the motion attached to them.

The Exposure:
Camera: Olympus E-520
Lens: Zuiko 12-60mm
Settings: F3.9 @ 1/20 sec ISO 400
Post-production: Aperture

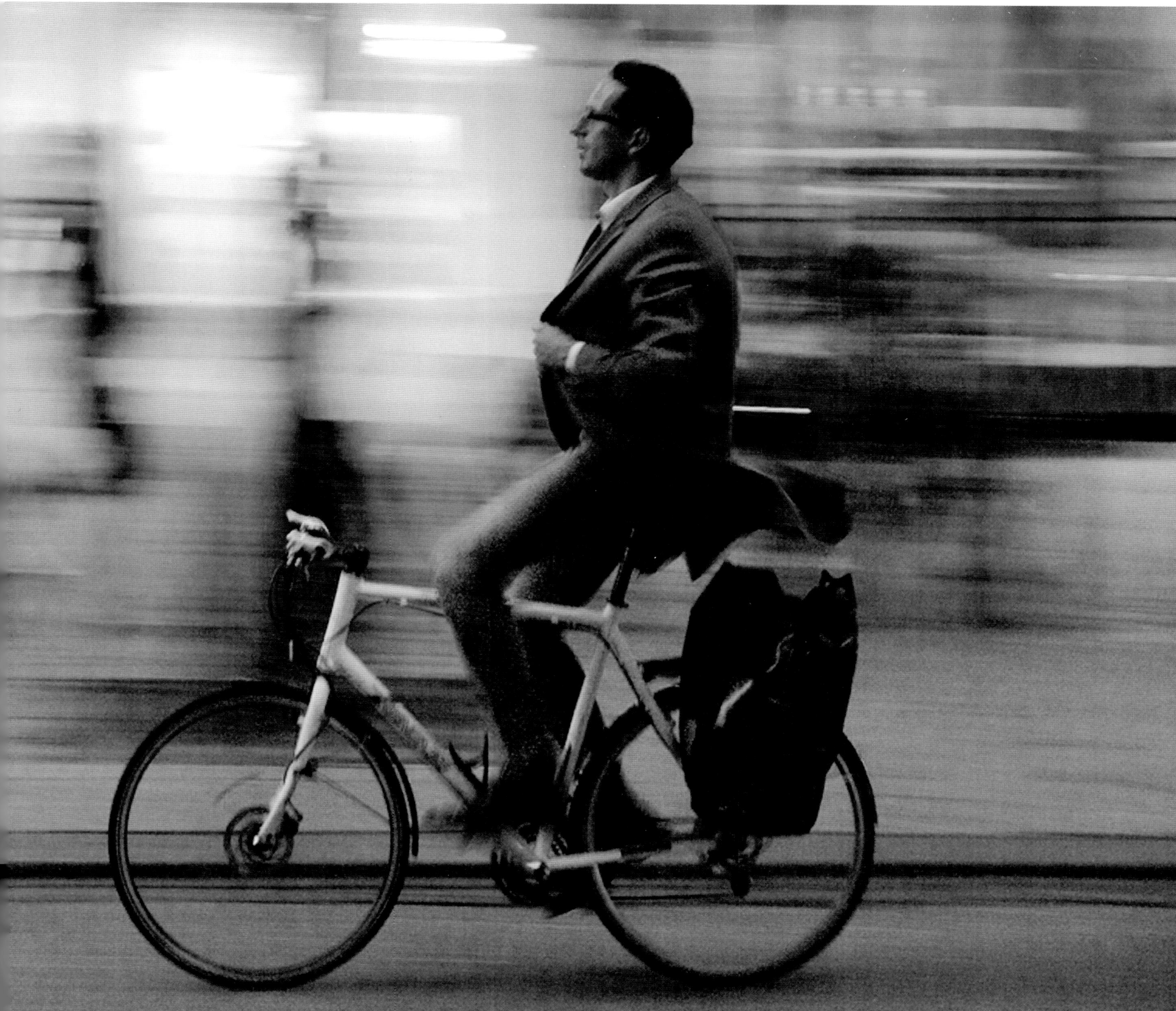

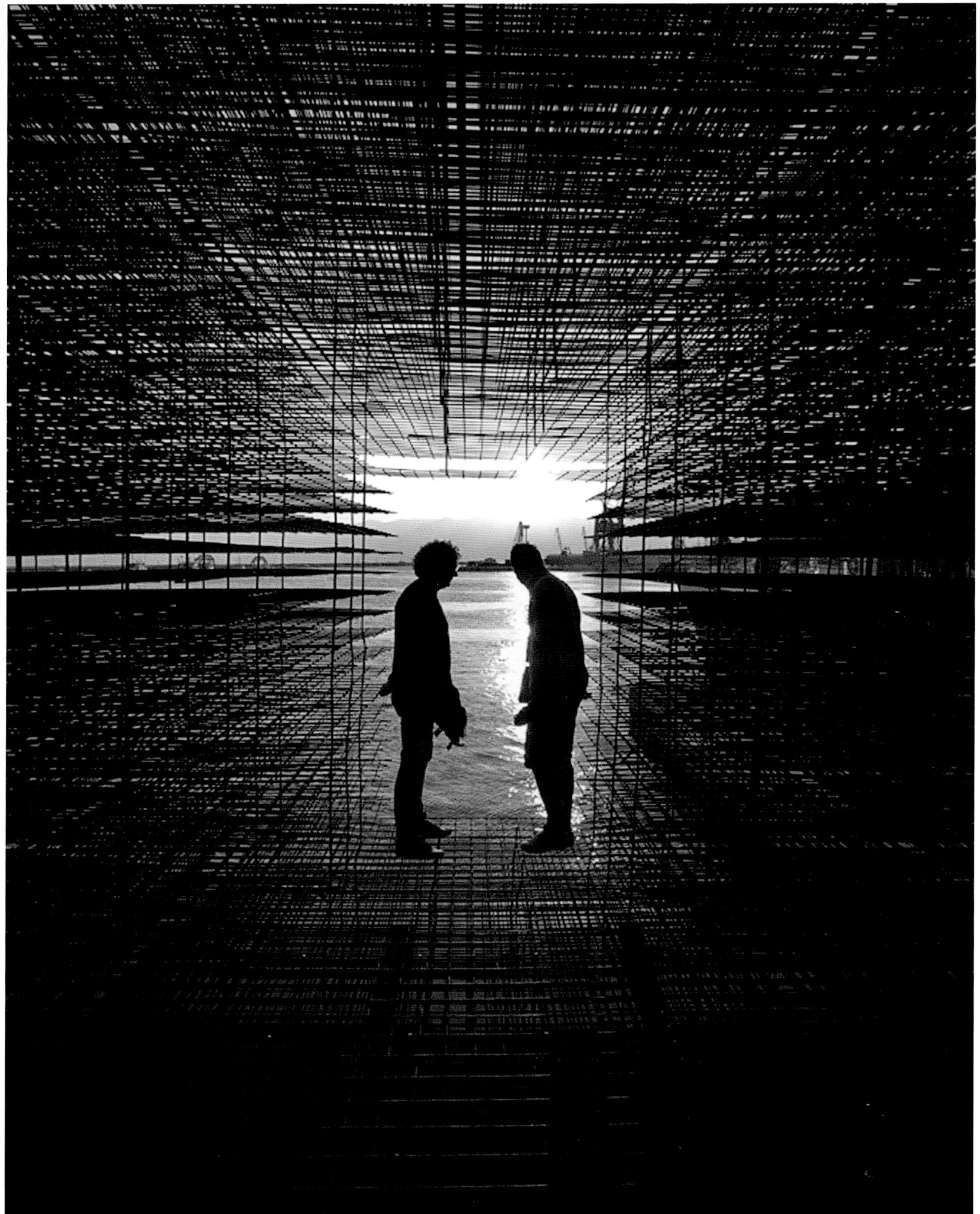

3rd Place Winner, 2010

Name: Aleksandar Tomulic, 44
Nationality: Croatian
Status: Professional
Photographer since: 2004
Favourite Camera of all Time: Canon 350D
Influences: Henri Cartier Bresson, Andre Kertesz, Stanko Abadzic

The Location: Rijeka, Croatia

The Story: This winning photo was taken inside the Croatian floating pavilion for the Biennial in Venice, which was situated in Rijeka harbour in August 2010. It was very interesting, constructed of lots of layers of iron nets. I picked the right lens (Canon 10-22), placed the people in the centre to show that 3D effect and took the photo.

The Exposure:
Camera: Canon 350D
Lens: Canon 10-22 mm
Settings: 10mm, F10, 1/250s, ISO 200
Post-production: conversion from RAW in black and white, contrast, sharpen

2009 WINNERS

1st Place Winner, 2009

Name: Ralf Pascual, 36
Nationality: Spanish
Status: Professional
Photographer since: 1997
Favourite Camera of all Time:
Rolley 35s, Nikon F4, Nikon D3s
Influences: Cristina Garcia Rodero,
Cartier Bresson, Robert Doisnau

The Location: Madrid, Spain

The Story: In a famous cafeteria, Gran Via in Madrid, on a rainy day in November, while talking with a friend, I noticed a window cleaner was cleaning a large window with determination. I then grabbed my camera and took several photos of the character.

The Exposure:
Camera: Nikon d300
Lens: Nikon 80-200 2,8
Settings: F4,5 V 1/100 sec ISO 400
Post-production: Photoshop and
Camera Raw

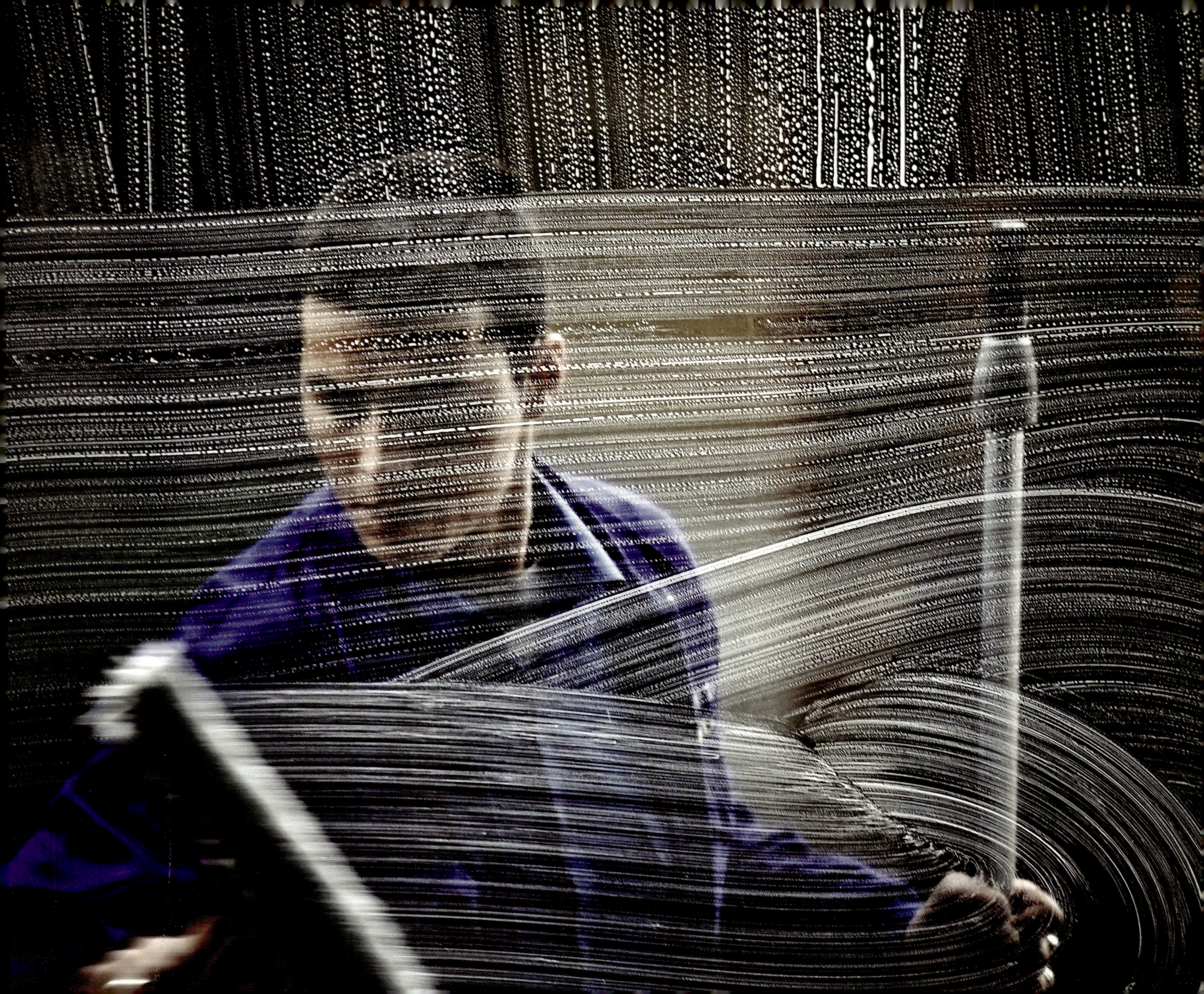

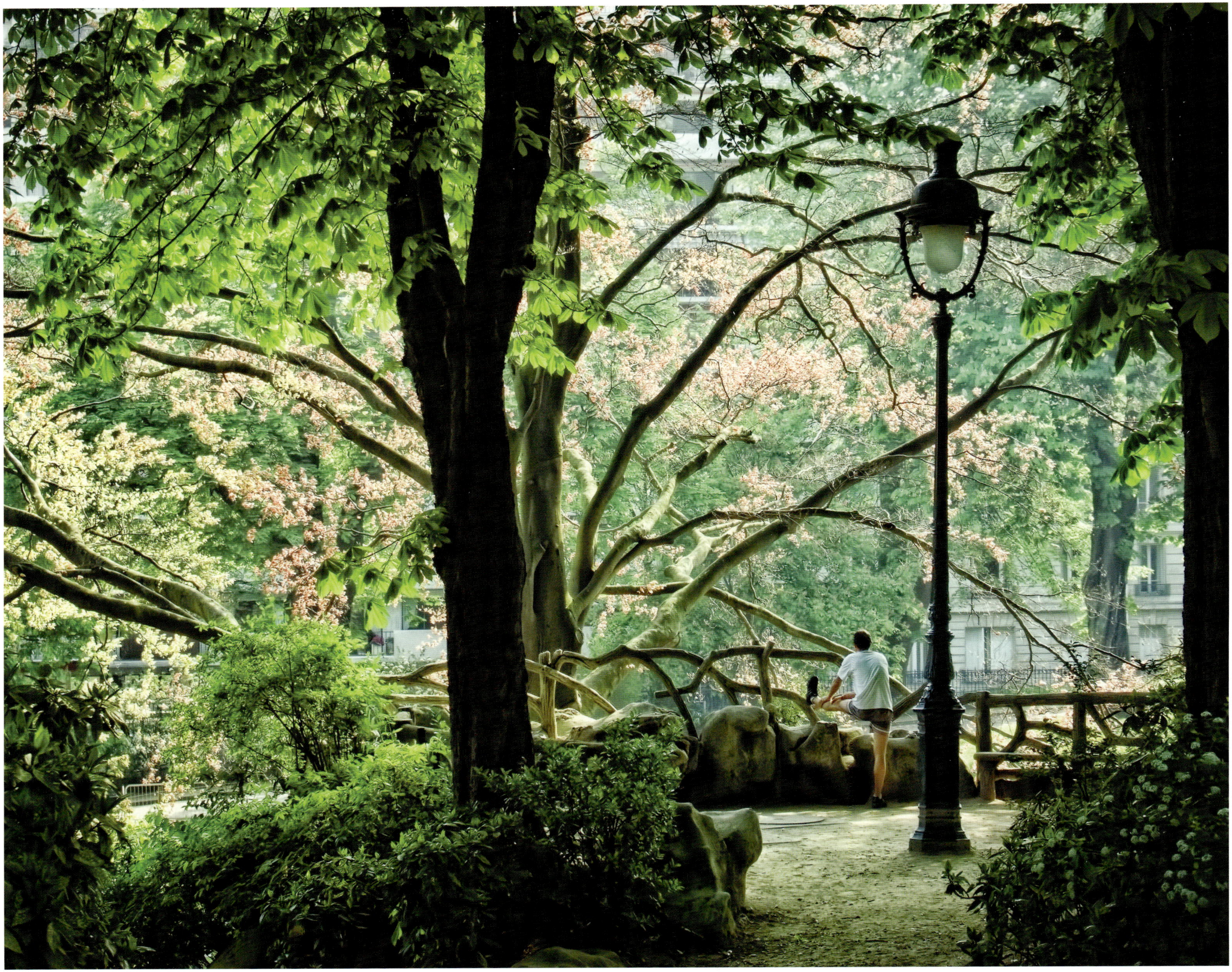

2nd Place Winner, 2009

Name: Jean-Marc Gargantiel, 55
Nationality: French
Status: Amateur
Photographer since: 1977
Favourite Camera of all Time: My eyes
Influences: Rainbows in the world

The Location: Paris, France

The Story: I was walking in the Parc Montsouris, a nice spring morning, when I saw this guy, surrounded by all these different colours and nature. I lifted my camera and shot it as fast as I could before he changed position.

The Exposure:
Camera: Konika Minolta A200
Lens: 18,4mm
Settings: F3,2 @1/60 sec ISO 50
Post-production: Photoshop

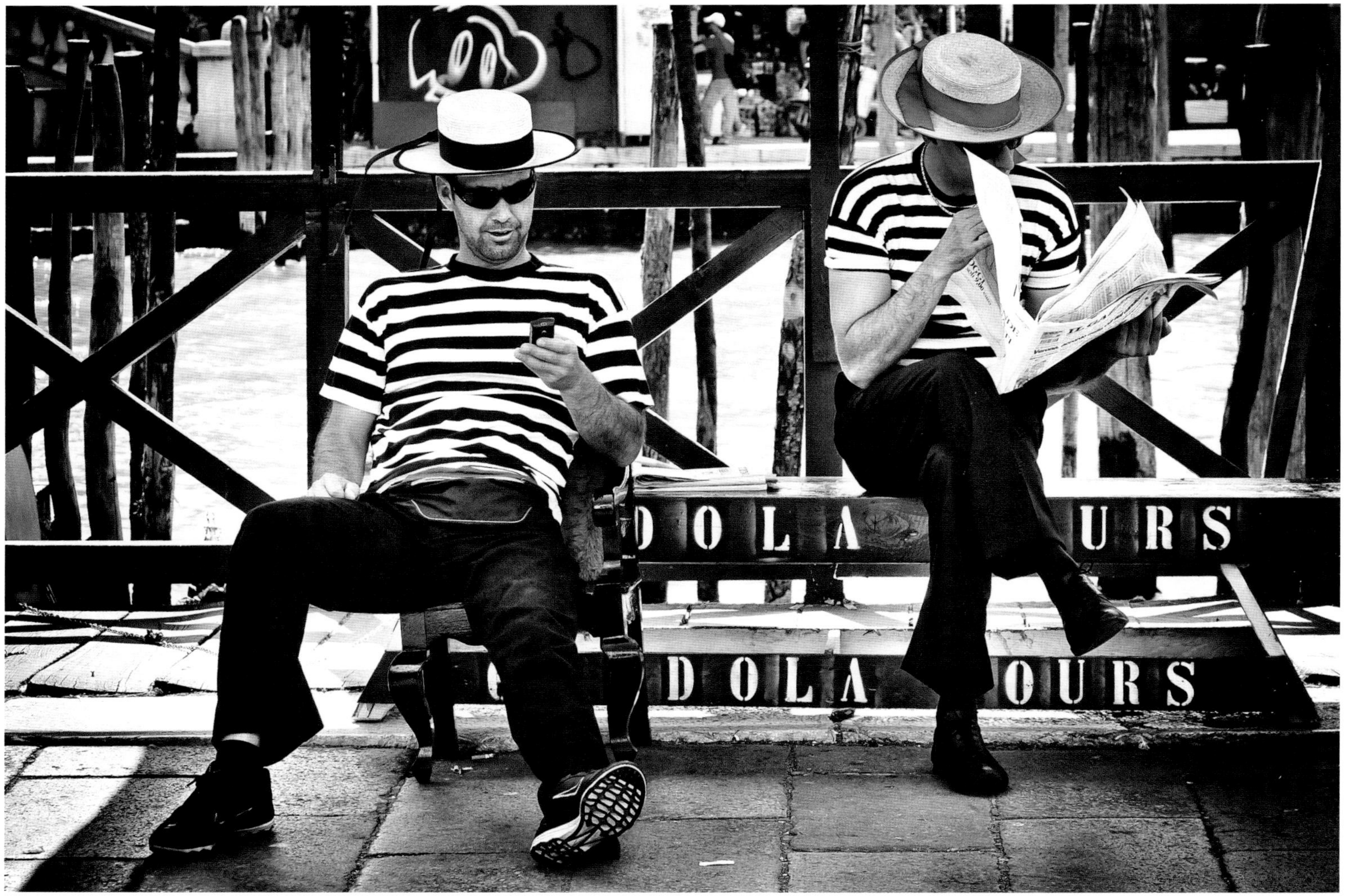
DOLA URS
DOLA OURS

3rd Place Winner, 2009

Name: Giancarlo Malandra, 43
Nationality: Italian
Status: Amateur
Photographer since: 2005
Favourite Camera of all Time:
Canon EOS series
Influences: Gianni Berengo Gardin, Henri Cartier-Bresson, Jean Gaumy, Sebastiao Salgado

The Location: Venice, Italy

The Story: I was looking for an image that wasn't the classic stereotype of a venetian gondolier.

The Exposure:
Camera: Canon EOS 350D
Lens: Canon EF 70-300 IS
Settings: F8 @ 1/160 sec ISO 100
Post-production: Photoshop, Lightroom

2008 WINNERS

1st Place Winner, 2008

Name: Charles Garnett, 60
Nationality: Scottish
Status: Amateur
Photographer since: 2000
Favourite Camera of all Time: Nikon D3
Influences: People and Streets

The Location: Glasgow, UK

The Story: I came across the dinner ladies having fun working together and decided to take a shot as I thought it fitted the remit for the competition.

The Exposure:
Camera: Nikon D40
Lens: Kit 18-55
Settings:F4 @ 1/600 sec ISO 400
Post-production: Photoshop

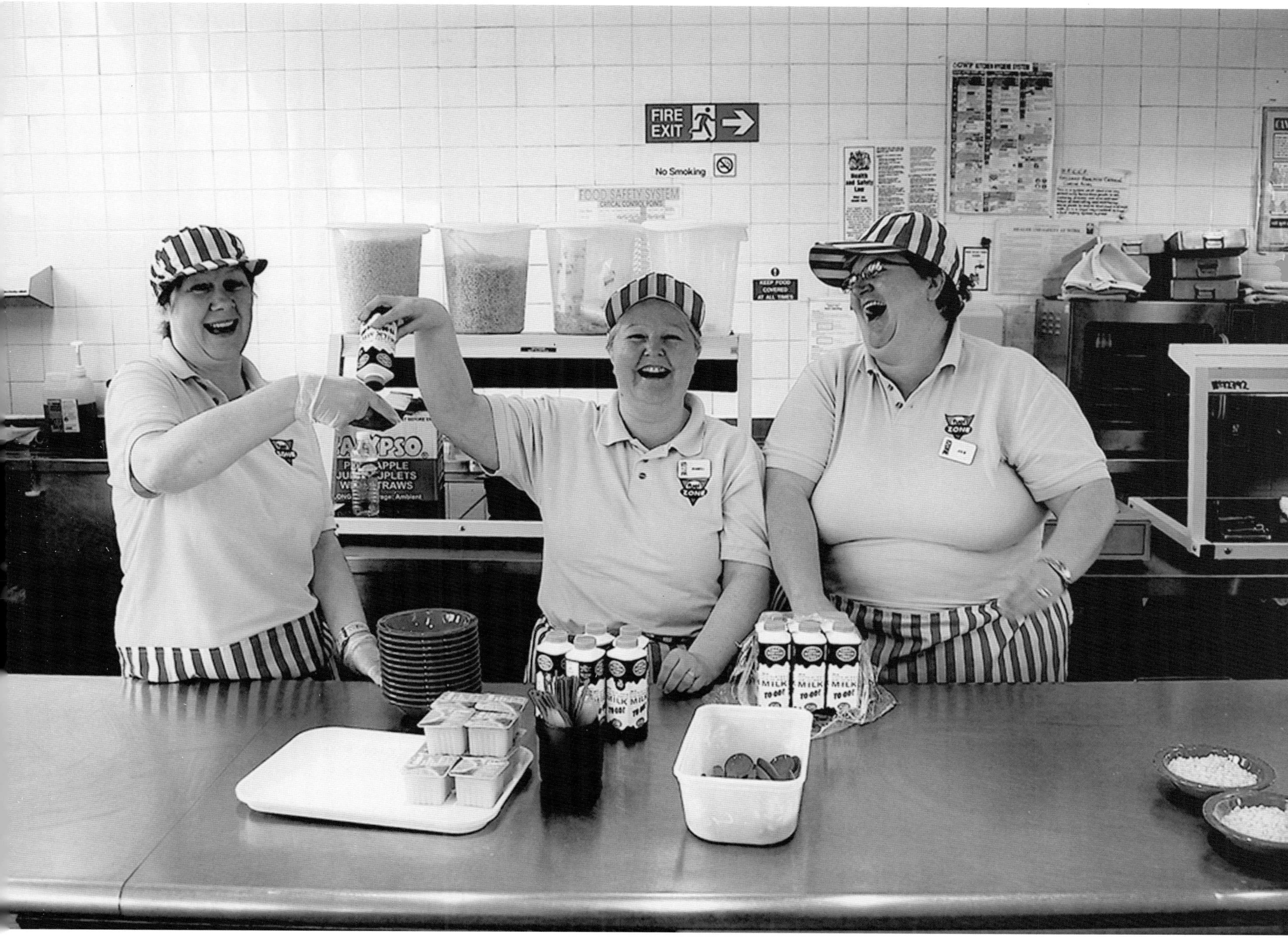
FIRE EXIT
No Smoking
FOOD SAFETY SYSTEM
KEEP FOOD COVERED AT ALL TIMES
MILK

2nd Place Winner, 2008
Name: Peter Swann, 32
Nationality: British
Status: Amateur
Photographer since: 2005
Favourite Camera of all Time:
Canon EOS 350D
Influences: Saul Leiter, Robert Frank, Stephen Shore, Gregory Crewdson

The Location: Wiltshire, UK

The Story: I love doing night photography because you have to stop and look, the tripod forces you to take stock. There is a footbridge that crosses a dual carriageway overlooking a petrol station, and I always thought it gave a good vantage point to look down. For me, 6pm was best represented by people's need to refuel their cars after work and the endless quest for Clubcard points.

The Exposure:
Camera: Canon EOS 350D
Lens: 17-85 mm F/4-5.6
Settings: F4 @ 1/2 sec ISO 100, -1 exposure bias
Post-production: Photoshop

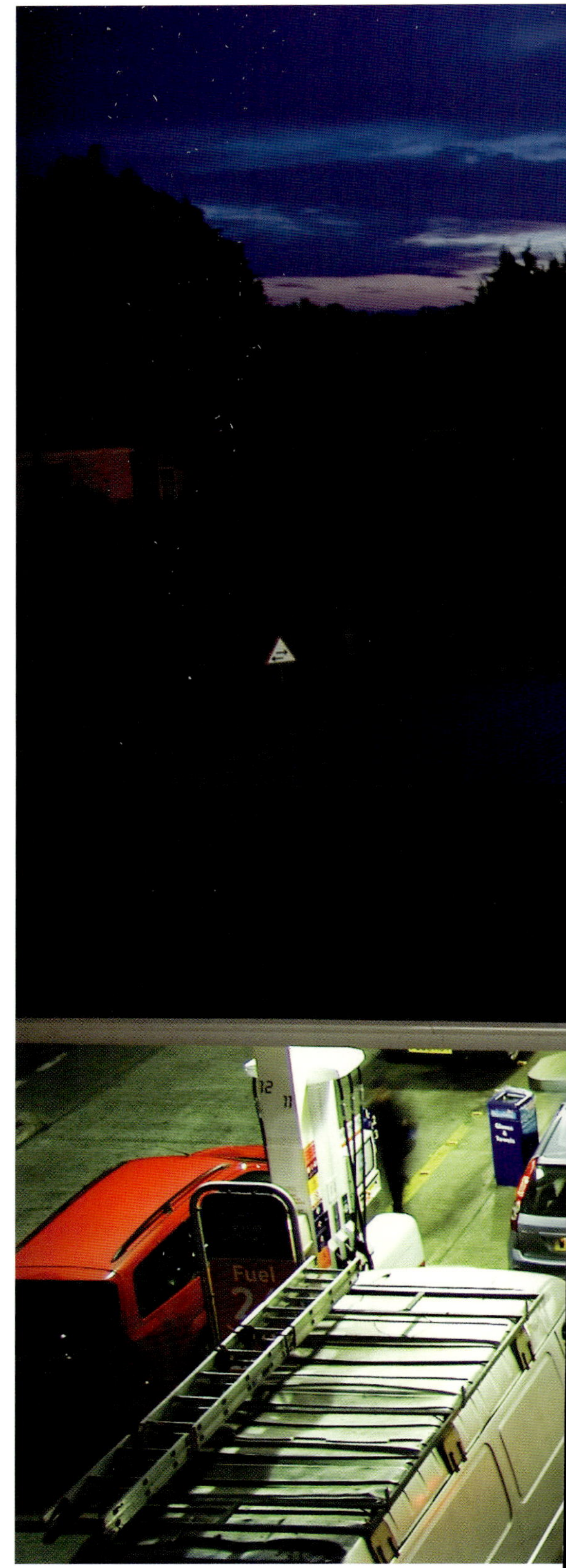

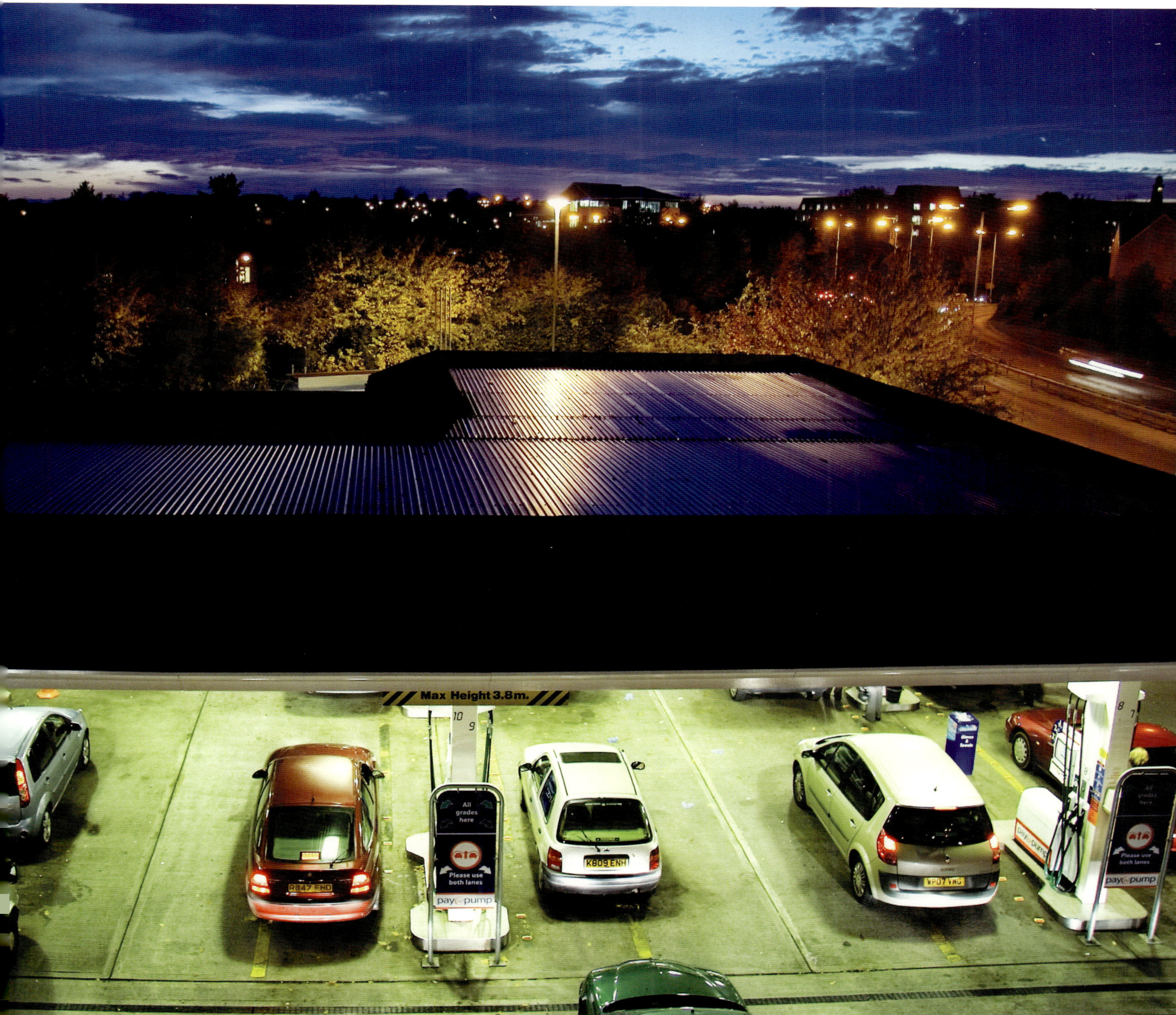
Max Height 3.8m.
All grades here
Please use both lanes

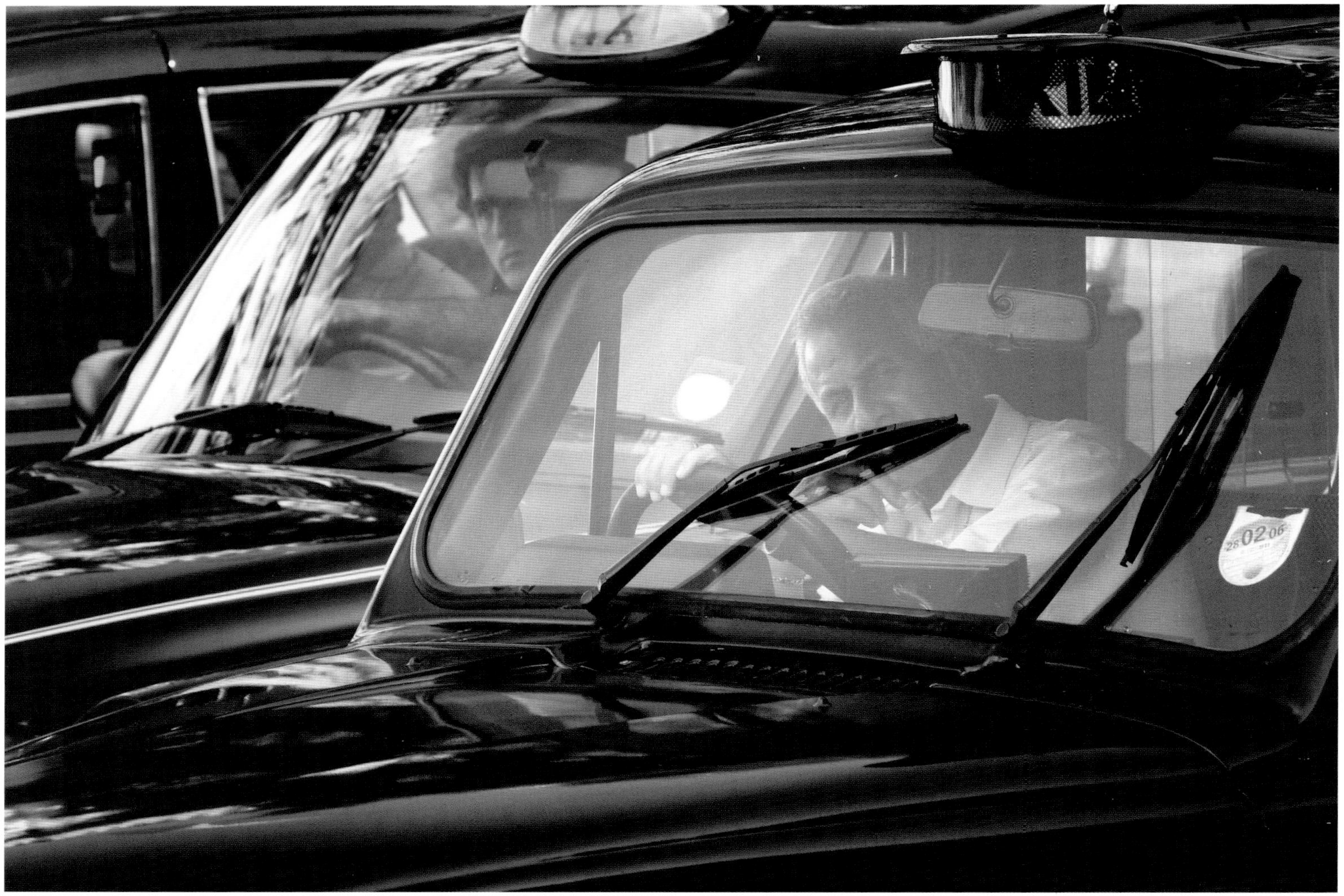

3rd Place Winner, 2008

Name: Warren Prasek, 38
Nationality: Australian
Status: Professional
Photographer since: 1998
Favourite Camera of all Time:
Canon EOS 20D
Influences: Stuart Clarke, Trey Ratcliff

The Location: London, UK

The Story: In the middle of a central London frenzied evening rush hour, I saw countless identical black cabs all going in the same direction on the road yet to a thousand different destinations, each with a driver and anonymous passengers inside. What were their stories? Where were they going? These parallel yet separate trajectories seemed a metaphor for the converging and diverging paths we all take in life... in a large city we live and work very close together, yet somehow we are more separate, distant and alone than ever before.

The Exposure:
Camera: Canon EOS 20D
Lens: EF 70-200 f/4L IS
Settings: F8 @ 1/320 sec ISO 400
Post-production: Photoshop

HOURLY WINNERS

Name: Liam Carroll, 32
Nationality: Irish
Status: Amateur
Photographer since: 2004
Favourite Camera of all Time:
Canon 5D Mk II
Influences: Steve McCurry, Dorothea Lange, Bob Dylan

The Location: Glasgow, UK

The Story: I was with a group of musicians, over in Scotland to pay tribute to a dear friend, through music and song. We were walking from one pub to the next on a cold October night, when i spotted this punk busking a clash song with great energy and attitude. A few of us befriended him and I asked him would he mind us taking a few snaps. I managed to get a few nice close ups, but the one I entered had an interesting composition, with a late night shopper returning home through a very intimidating alleyway.

The Exposure:
Camera: Nikon D 60
Lens: 32 mm
Settings: F84.8@ 1/200 sec ISO 800
Post-production: Photoshop, Lightroom

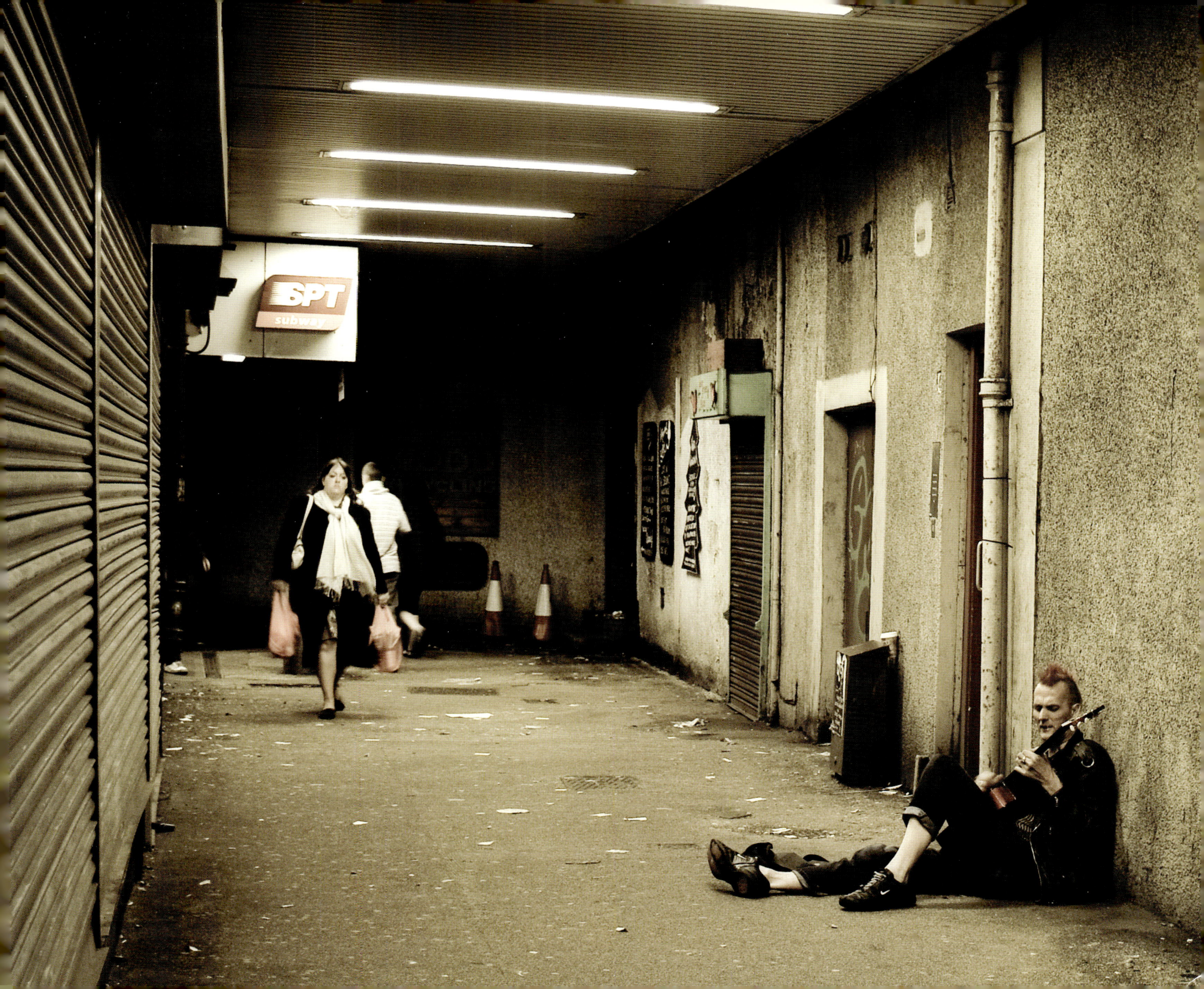
SPT
subway

Name: Georges De Kinder, 40
Nationality: Belgian
Status: Professional
Photographer since: 1991
Favourite Camera of all Time: Hasselblad
Influences: Rene Descartes, Ed Weston, My Mother

The Location: Brussels, Belgium

The Story: It's a photograph I've shot for a personal editorial project about the stations.

The Exposure:
Camera: Nikon D3X
Lens: 24 mm tilt & shift
Settings: F8 @ 3 sec ISO 200
Post-production: Nikon Capture, Photoshop

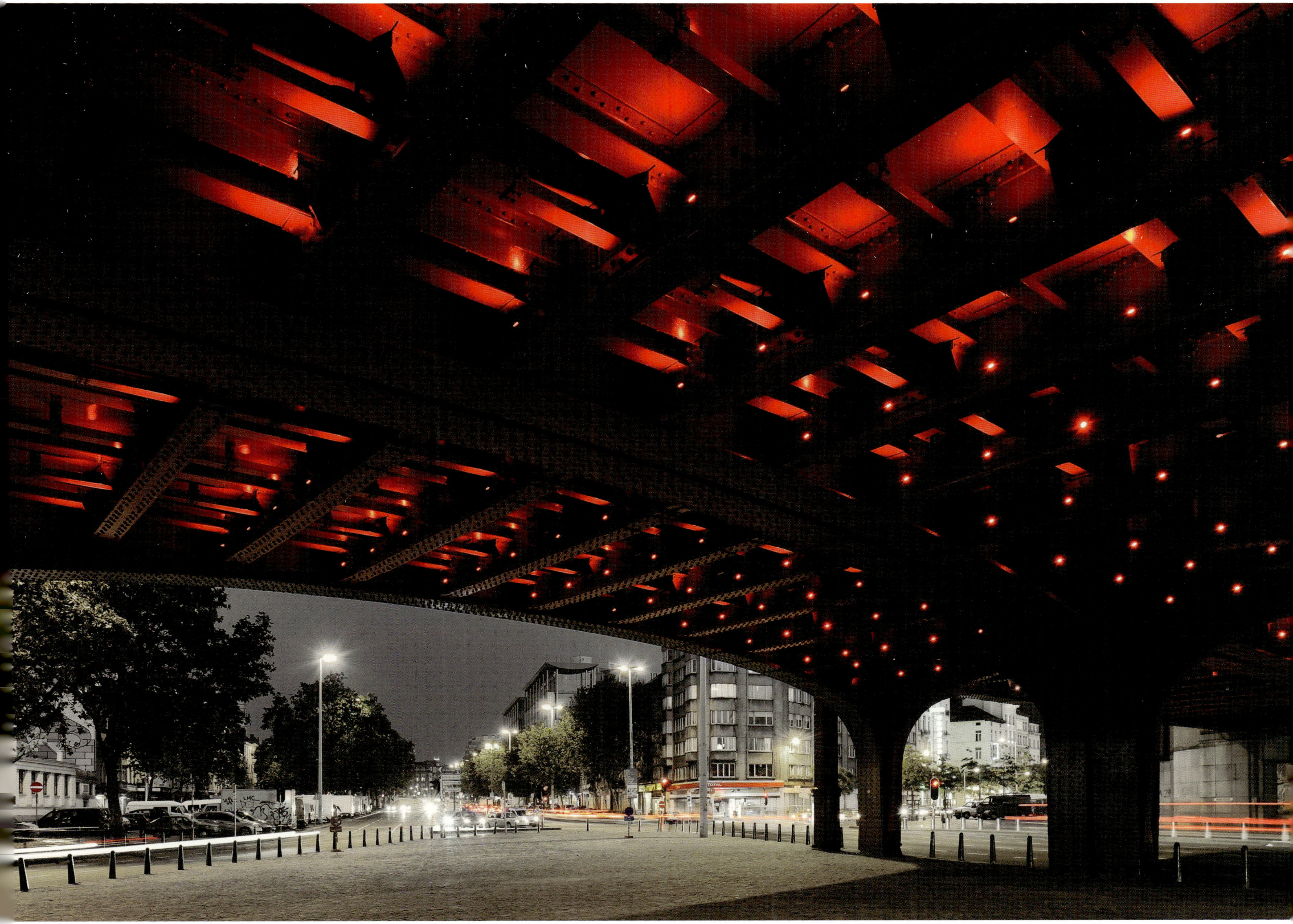

Name: Linda Wride, 18
Nationality: British
Status: Amateur
Photographer since: 2004
Favourite Camera of all Time: Nikon D300
Influences: Receiving feedback to my images has influenced my work.

The Location: Glasgow, UK

The Story: It was the combination of colours (yellow wall panels, bright orange jacket and blue cleaning machine) that initially caught my eye. I can remember being mid-conversion with friends, then suddenly taking off and half-walking, half-running, crab fashion along the platform opposite, trying to capture the figure framed between columns, before he was obscured by passing trains.

The Exposure:
Camera: Pentax *ist DL2
Settings: F/6.7 ISO 800
Post-production: Photoshop

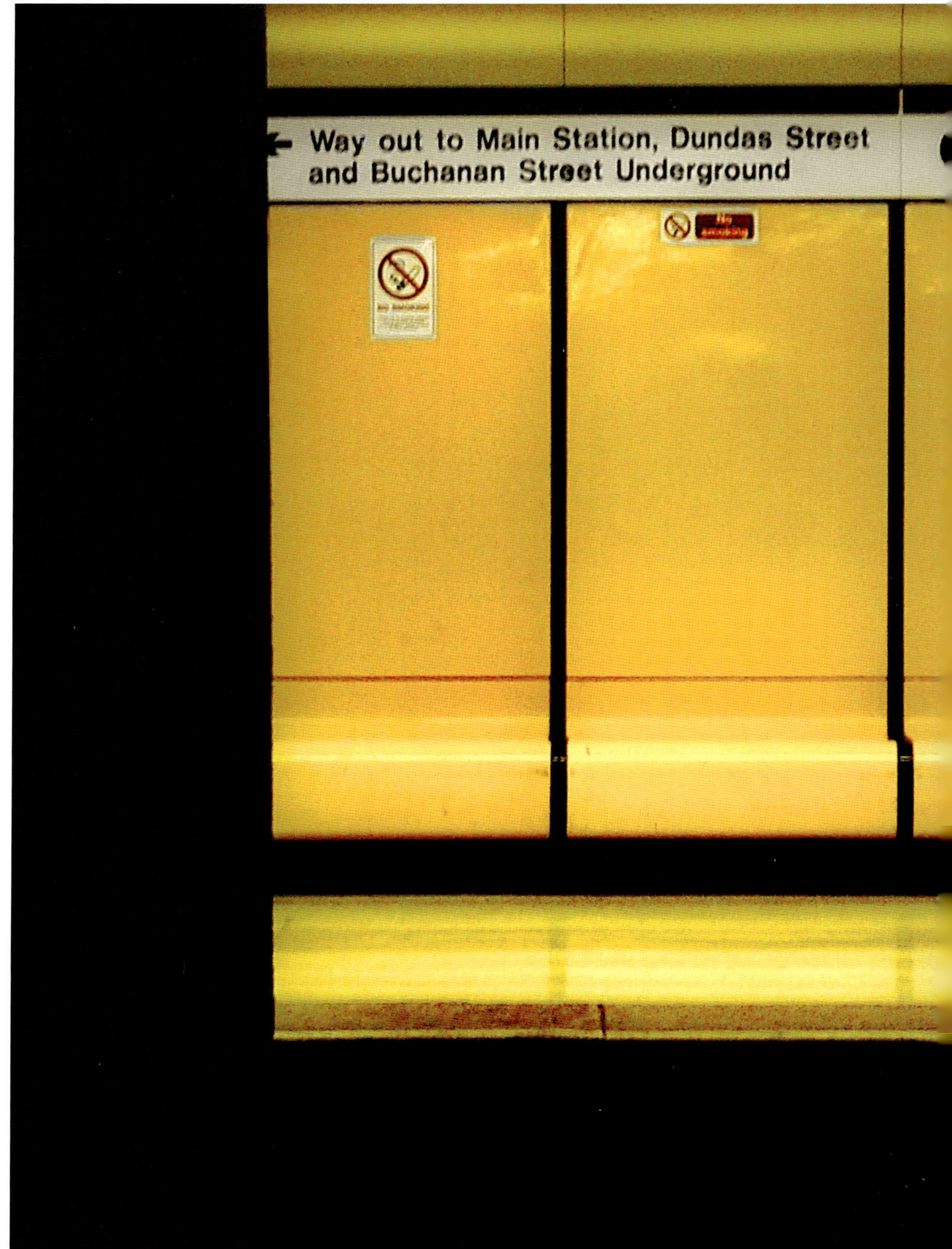

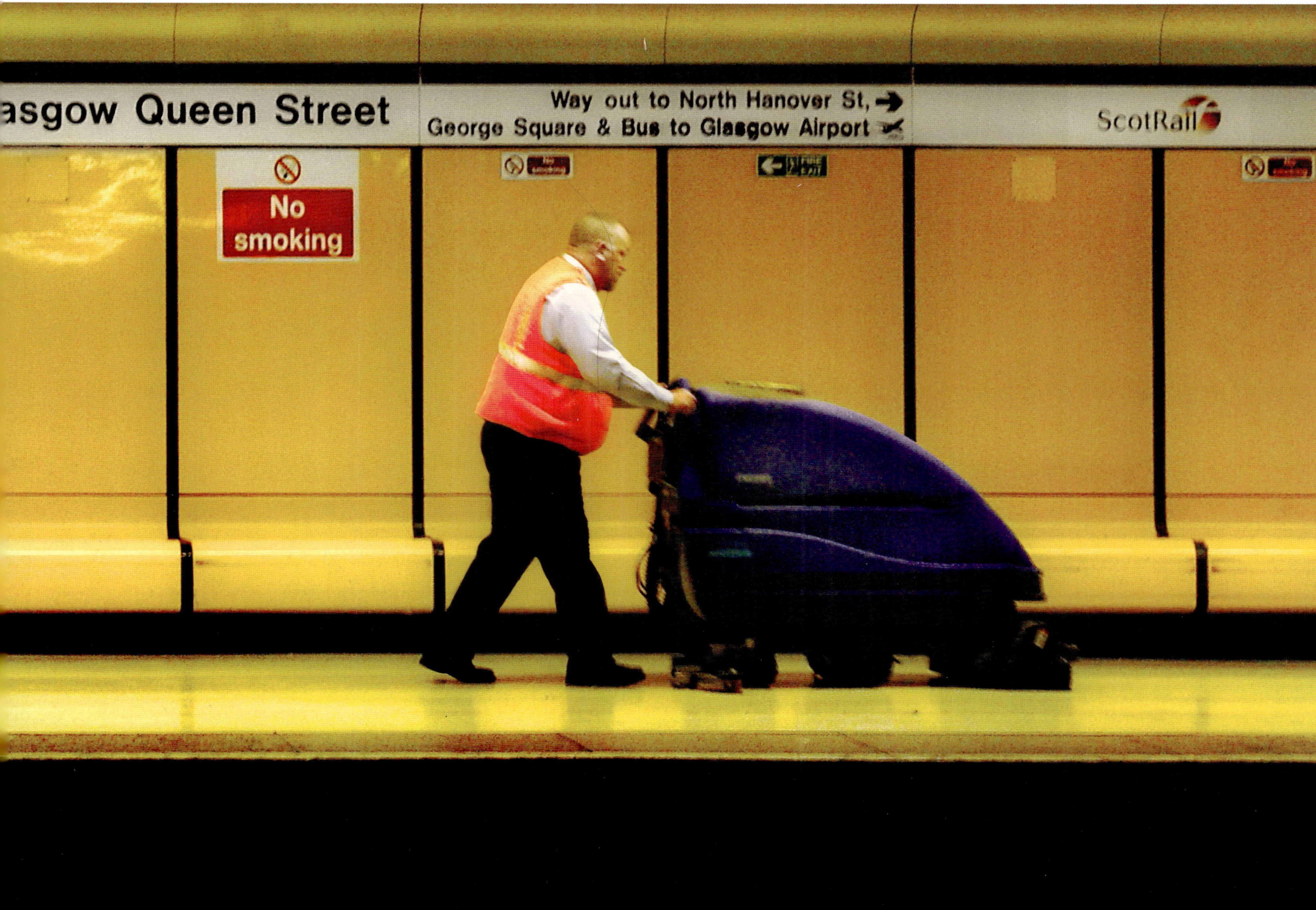
asgow Queen Street
Way out to North Hanover St,
George Square & Bus to Glasgow Airport
ScotRail
No smoking

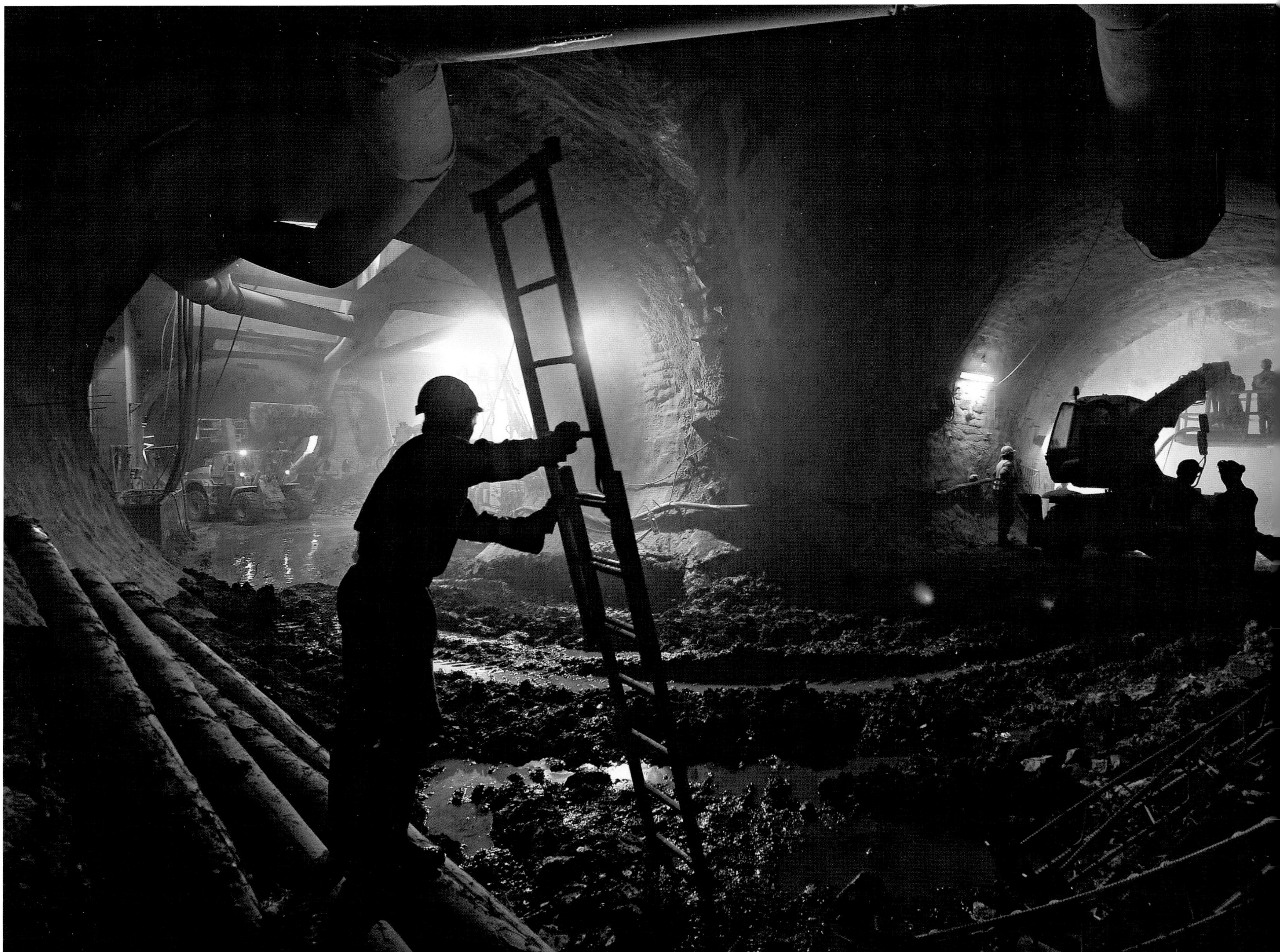

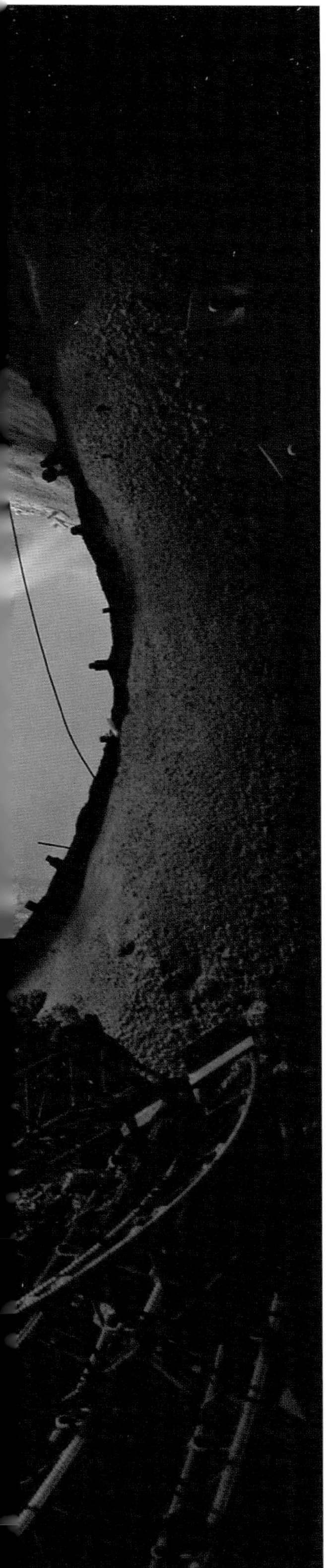

Name: Vanik Zoltán, 35
Nationality: Hungarian
Status: Professional
Photographer since: 2007
Favourite Camera of all Time: Nikon D3
Influences: André Kertész

The Location: Budapest, Hungary

The Story: The contrast between the bright lighting and the tunnel's natural darkness captured the silhouettes of the men and their machinery at work.

The Exposure:
Camera: Nikon D3
Lens: Nikkor 14-24 F:2,8 (at 15mm)
Settings: F5,6 @ 1/20 sec ISO 800
Post-production: Photoshop

Name: Benoît De Greift, 32
Nationality: Belgian
Status: Amateur
Photographer since: 2004
Favourite Camera of all Time:
Canon EOS 350D
Influences: Cham Maddoz, Javier Arcenillas

The Location: Amsterdam, Holland

The Story: I was staying in a hotel that reminded me of an illuminated spaceship at night.

The Exposure:
Camera: Canon EOS 350D
Lens: 50mm F/1.8
Settings: F/1.8 1/50 ISO 200
Post-production: Photoshop

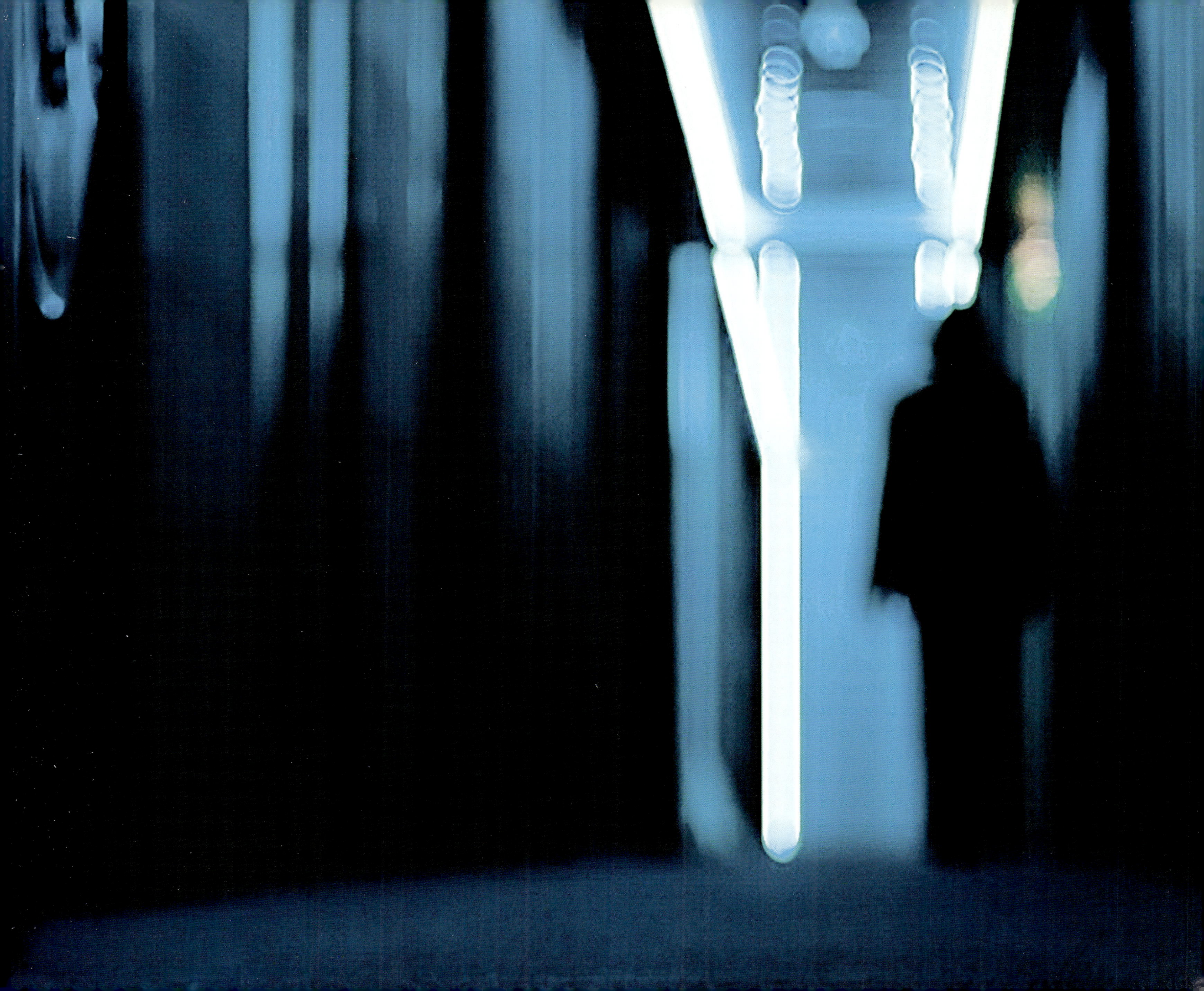

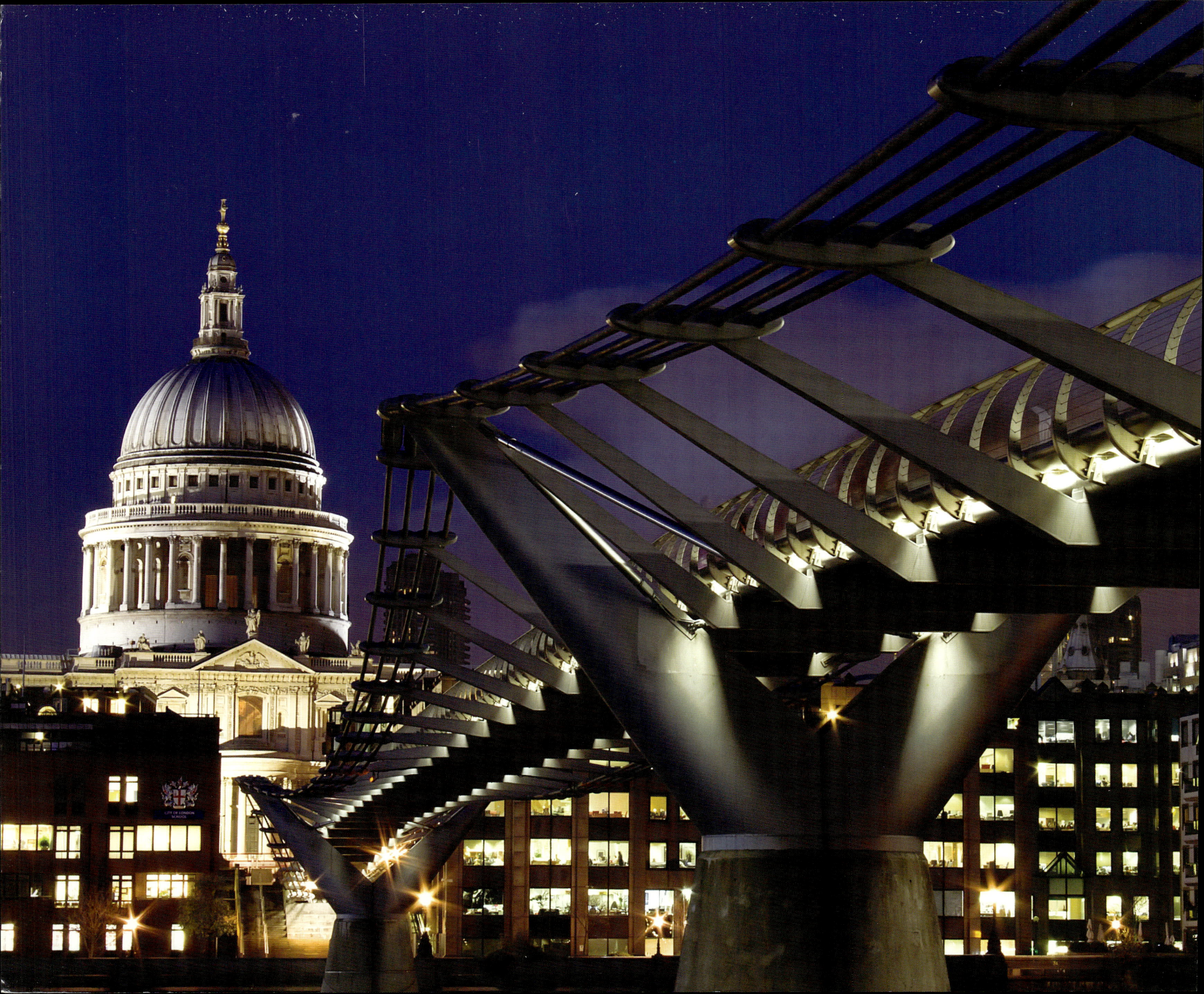

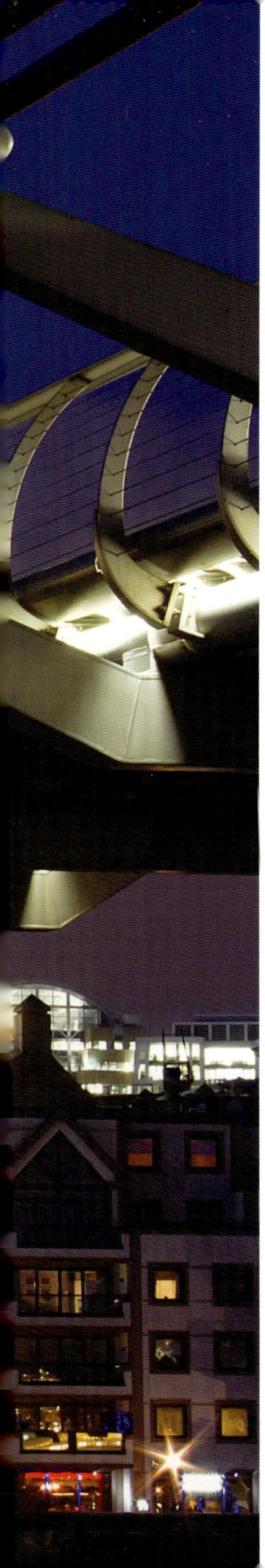

Name: Arron Gent, 33
Nationality: English
Status: Amateur
Photographer since: 2010
Favourite Camera of all Time:
Canon 5D Mark II
Influences: Trey Ratcliff, Rick Salmon, Luciano Bonacini

The Location: London, UK

The Story: This picture was taken in London, by the Millenium Bridge. The inspiration behind the photo itself was that I wanted to get the old and the new in one shot with the bridge being the new and St Paul's, the old, rising in the background. The inspiration also comes from the fact I work in London and have done for several years and it's easy to miss all of what's around you, the deep history of London and all of it's beautiful architecture! The plan is to return and capture many other parts of London that people like me take for granted.

The Exposure:
Camera: Canon 550D
Lens: EF-S18-55mm f/3.5-5.6 IS
Settings: F22 - 30sec exposure - ISO 100
Post-production: Photoshop

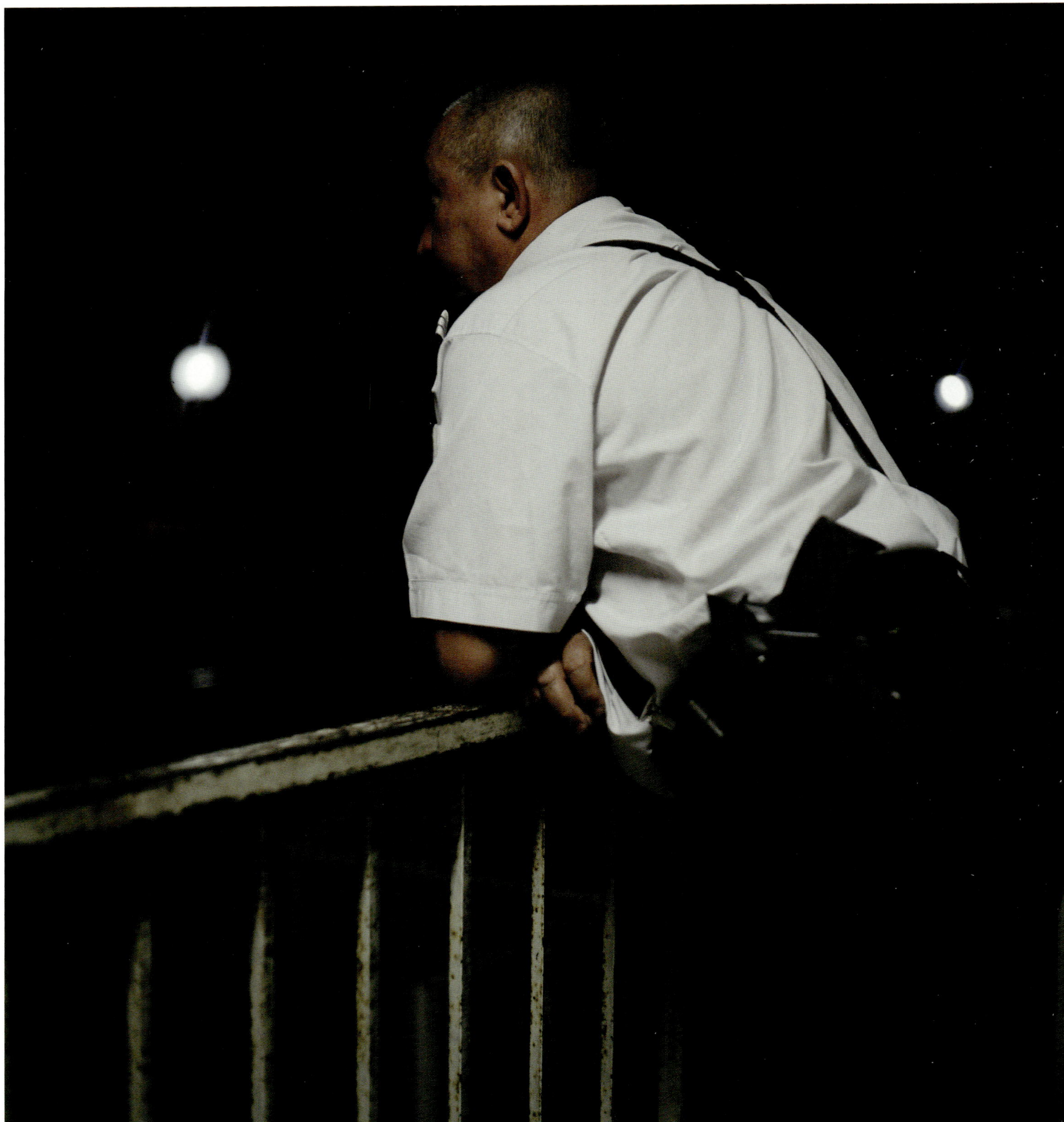

Name: Lucile Chombart de Lauwe 25
Nationality: French
Status: Professional
Photographer since: 2004
Favourite Camera of all Time: Mamyia C330
Influences: Denis Dailleux, Diane Arbus, Jacob Riis, Lewis Hine, Peter Hugo

The Location: Arles, France

The Story: This image was taken as part of a documentary project on night workers. This image depicts a policeman just taking a break during a calm night shift.

The Exposure:
Camera: Mamyia c330
Lens: 80mm F2,8
Settings: F2,8 1/15 sec ISO 400
Post-production: Photoshop

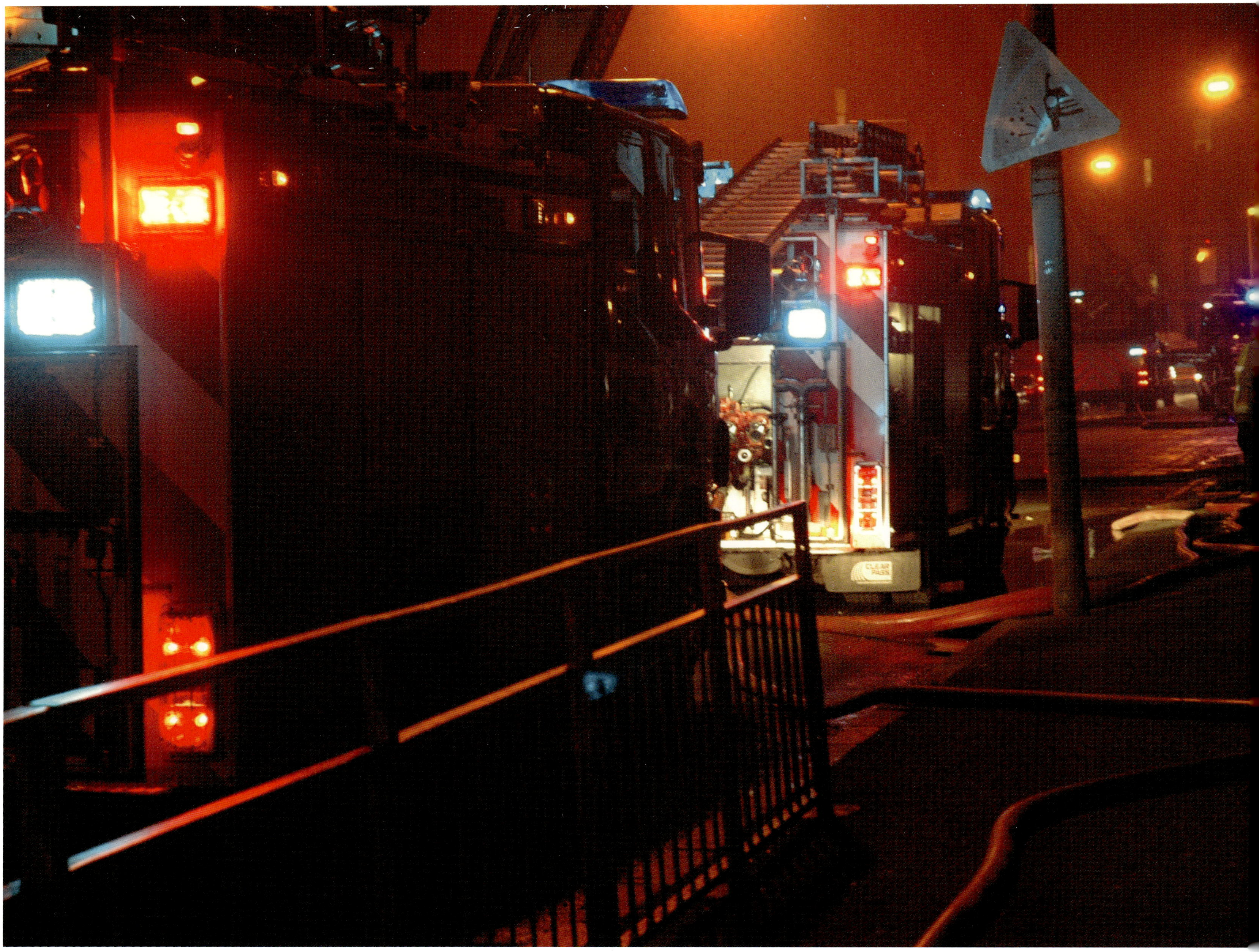
CLEAR
PASS

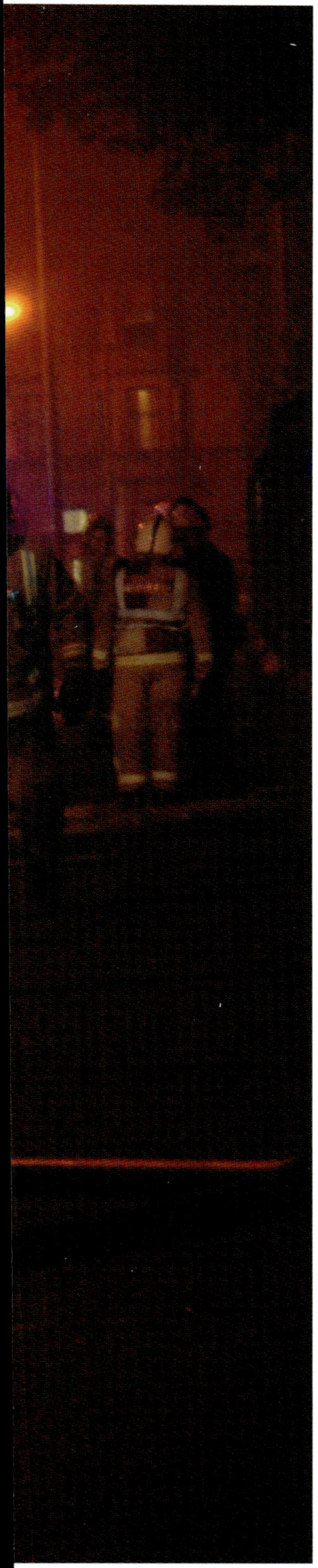

Name: June Toner, 53
Nationality: Canadian
Status: Amateur
Photographer since: 1968
Favourite Camera of all Time: Mamiya 645
Influences: Henri Cartier-Bresson, Annie Leibovitz

The Location: Glasgow, UK

The Story: A fearsome fire had just been extinguished in a derelict building, when the attending firemen started to clear up for the night... just another day at the office for them.

The Exposure:
Camera: Pentax *ist DL2
Lens: 18-70mm
Settings: F3.5 @ 1/60 sec ISO 1600

Name: Pablo Pacheco, 30
Nationality: Spanish
Status: Professional
Photographer since: 2009
Favourite Camera of all Time:
Canon 5D Mark II
Influences: Eugenio Recuenco,
Rafa Gallar

The Location: Palma, Mallorca

The Story: Whenever I was in the laundrette, there was always a girl there, smoking, looking bored. One day I brought my camera with me and the result is this shot.

The Exposure:
Camera: Canon 5D Mark II
Lens: 50 mm / F1.8
Settings: F2.5 @ 1/80 sec ISO 640
Post-production: Photoshop

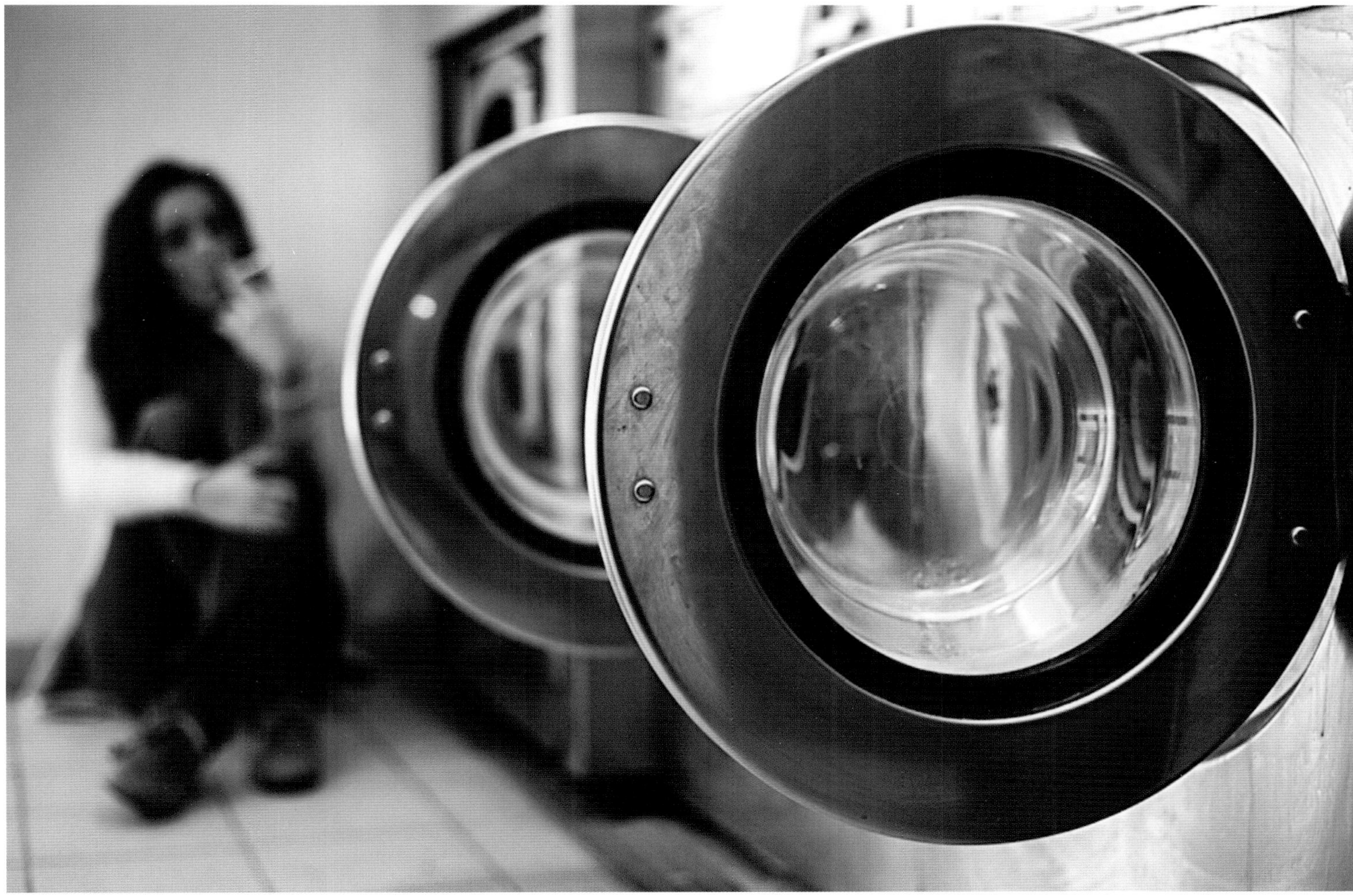

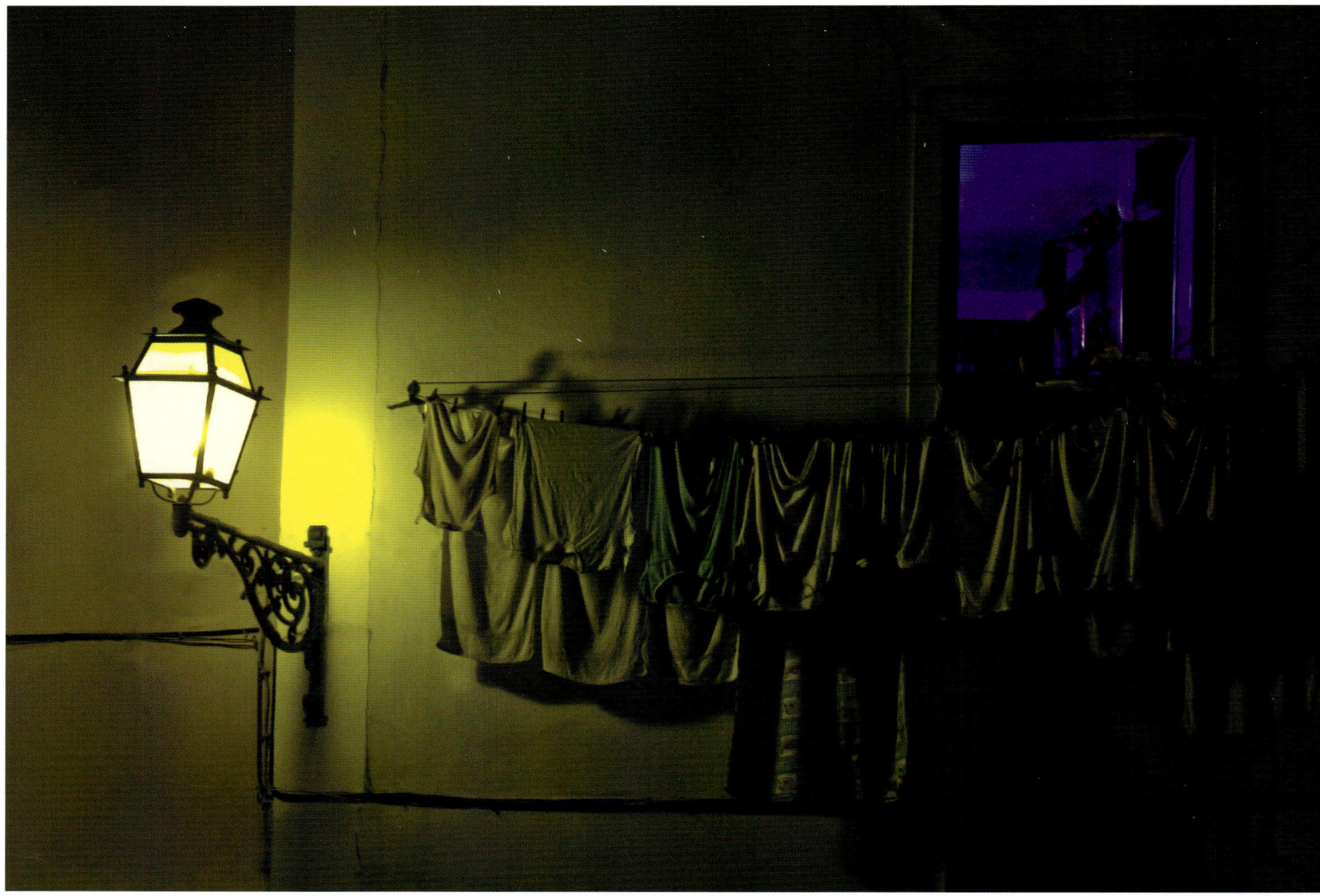

Name: Vitor Gomes, 62
Nationality: Portuguese
Status: Amateur
Photographer since: 1975
Favourite Camera of all Time: Olympus E-30
Influences: Olivier Pasquier, Hugues de Wurstemberger, Samuel Bollendorf

The Location: Lisbon (Alfama) – Portugal

The Story: I captured this detail of life in Alfama, one of the oldest neighborhoods of Lisbon. Visiting at night is a real surprise. The charm of its buildings stands out among the contrast of the shadows and faint lights.

The Exposure:
Camera: Olympus E-500
Lens: Olympus 14-54 @ 52 mm
Settings: F7, 1, 1/5 sec, ISO 320
Post-production: Photoshop

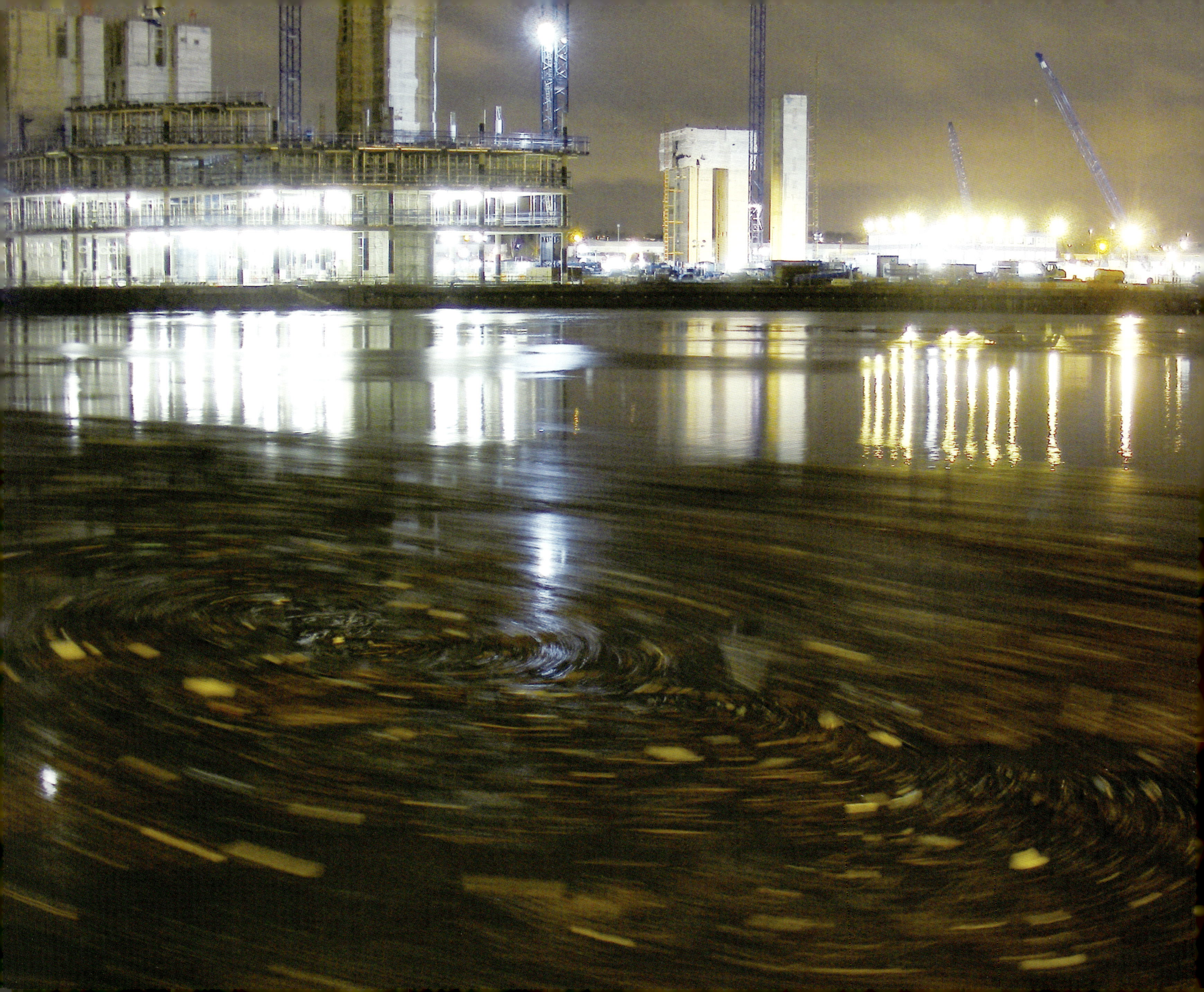

Name: Tom Fairclough, 51
Nationality: British
Status: Amateur
Photographer since: 1975
Favourite Camera of all Time: Olympus OM1
Influences: Vermeer, Hopper, Stanley Spencer

The Location: Manchester, UK

The Story: I was looking around for shots when I saw this fast swirling pile of timber, very quiet, very dark, very weird. This completed area will soon be one of the best known sights in Britain.

The Exposure:
Camera: Fujifilm S5700
Lens: Fujinon 6.3-63mm
Settings: F3.5 @ 4 seconds ISO 64
Post-production: Photoshop CS4, unsharp mask and curves

Name: António Leão de Sousa, 52
Nationality: Portuguese
Status: Amateur
Photographer since: 1980
Favourite Camera of all Time:
Canon EOS 7D
Influences: Joel Santos,
David Nightingale, Joe Cornish

The Location:
Vala do Carregado, Portugal

The Story: This picture captures the power station of Carregado, about 40 km from Lisbon, near the north bank of the Tejo river, in a place called Vala do Carregado. Returning home after another long day at work, I noticed the wind forms modelling the steam coming out of one of the cooling towers in a thermal power station. I prepared the tripod, and after taking some long exposures without being able to balance the high-lights, I chose to set on the theme that drew my attention, the steam.

The Exposure:
Camera: Canon EOS 7D
Lens: Canon EFS 15-85 F3.5-5.6
Settings: F/4.5 19/1 sec ISO 320 Focal length 35mm
Post-production: Lightroom and Photoscape

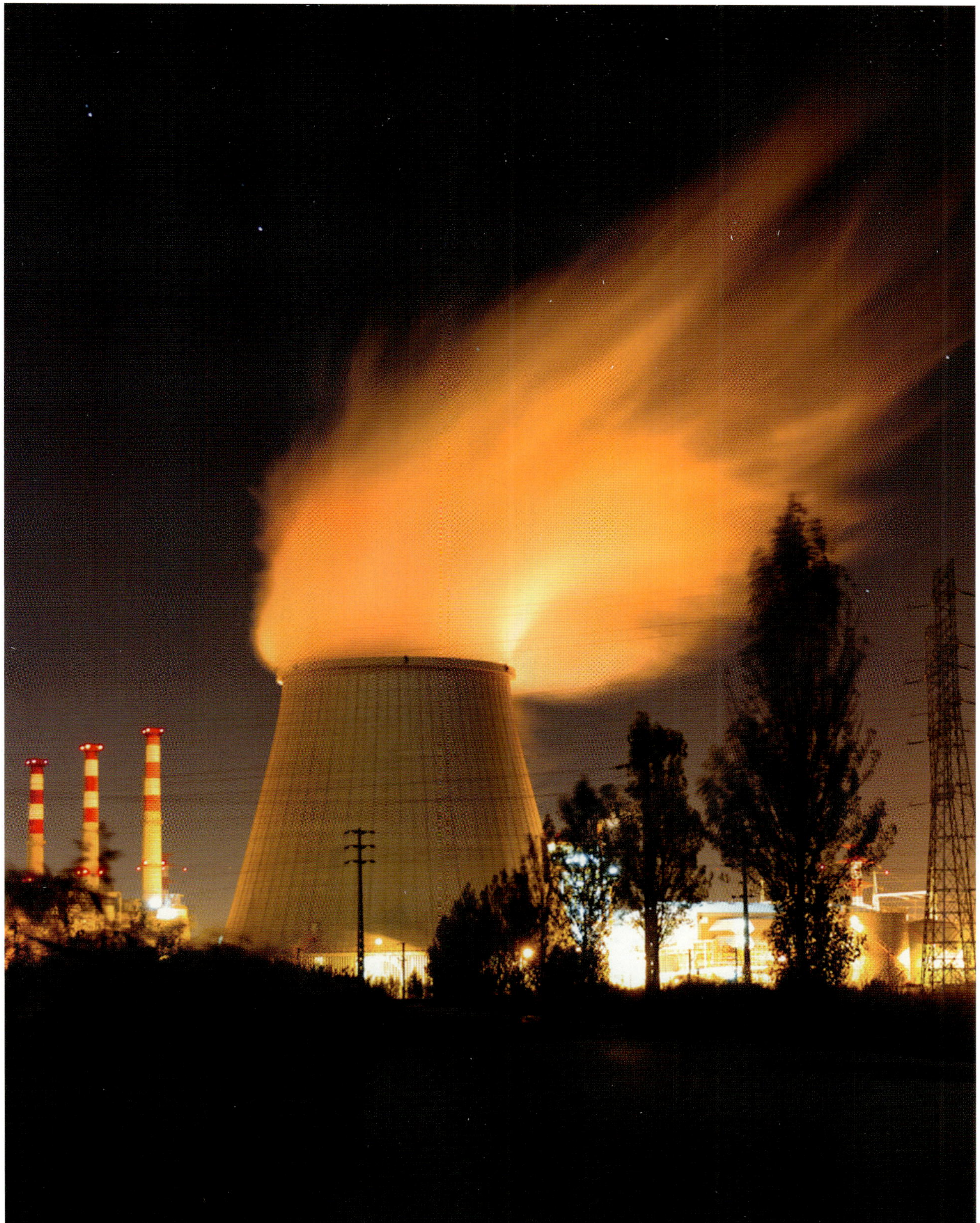

Name: Shadi Eideh, 37
Nationality: Jordanian
Status: Professional
Photographer since: 2005
Favourite Camera of all Time:
My Canon 5D Mark II
Influences: Helmut Newton, Gregory Heisler, Chase Jarvis, Joe Mcnally, David Hobby

The Location: Amman, Jordan

The Story: I remember that sleepless night clearly. I was beginning to learn photography and remember feeling guilty for not shooting enough that summer. I went out on the balcony to relax and enjoy the cool summer breeze. 5 minutes later I ran inside and propped my camera on a cheap tripod and took the picture. Although I don't do a lot of landscapes, this photo remains a favorite of mine.

The Exposure:
Camera: Nikon D70
Lens: Sigma 18-200 f/3.5-6.3
Settings: F32 @ 39 sec ISO 200
Post-production: Photoshop

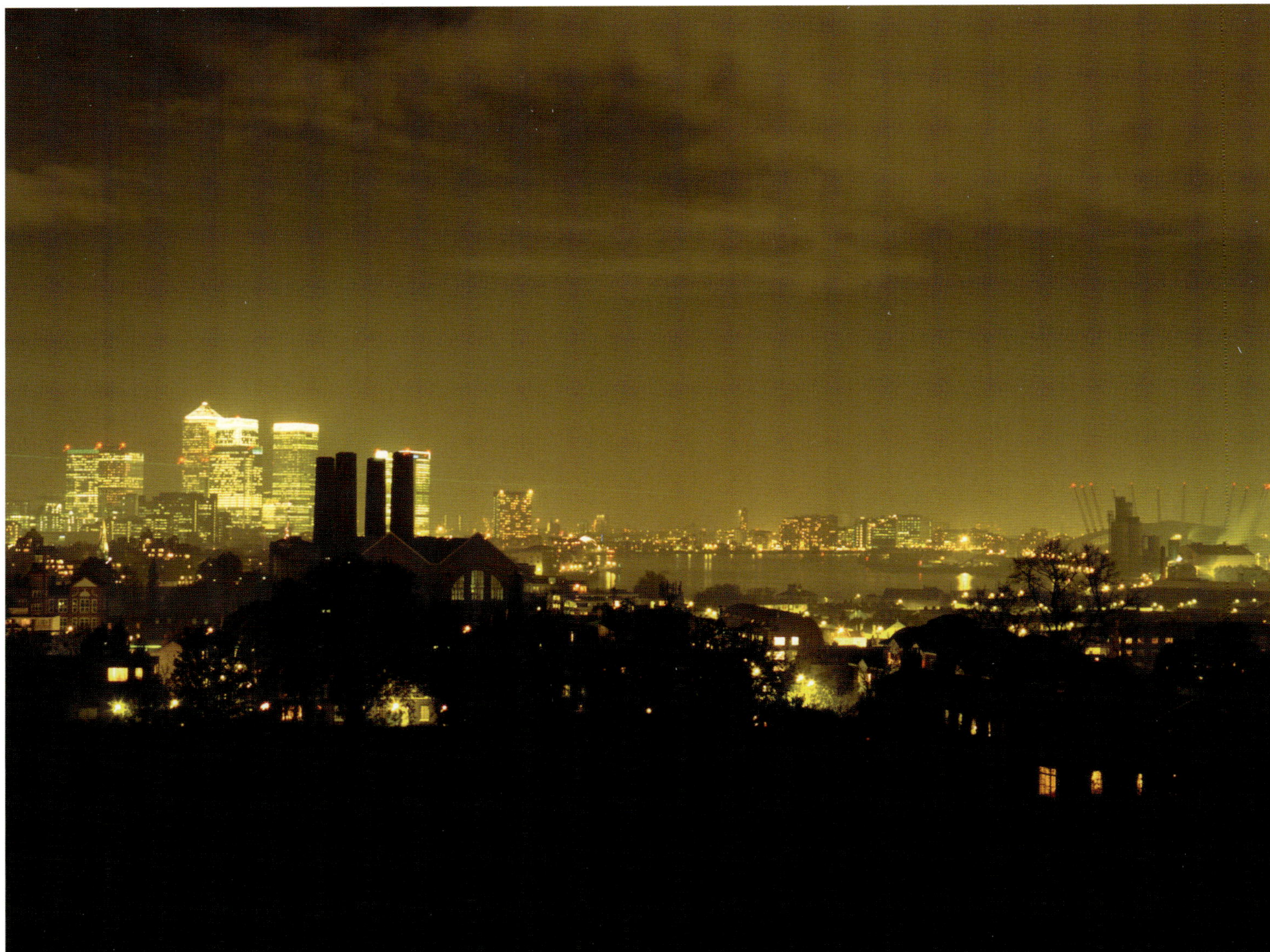

Name: Mark Wilkinson, 44
Nationality: Scottish
Status: Documentary Photographer
Photographer since: 2000
Favourite Camera of all Time: Lieca M6
Influences: Robert Frank, Walker Evans, Diane Arbus, Richard Avedon

The Location: Greenwich, London, UK

The Story: I took this shot from the top of Greenwich Park next to the Observatory. The park is locked at night so I had to jump over the fence to get this spectacular viewpoint. The sky is lit up by the city lights, and the towers of Canary Wharf in the background are mirrored by the obsolete power station in the foreground. To me this marks the transition of the industrial age to the financial age.

The Exposure:
Camera: Pentax 645
Lens: 50mm
Settings: F11 @ 15 seconds ISO 800
Post-production: Photoshop

Name: Áron Süveg, 33
Nationality: Hungarian
Status: Professional
Photographer since: 2004
Favourite Camera of all Time: Nikon D200
Influences: Steve McCurry, Robert Capa, Henri Cartier-Bresson,

The Location: Budapest, Hungary

The Story: This photo was taken after a big party in Budapest. I was on my way back home to the castle district and stopped for a while to watch the sunrise. It was really nice to see how different the city is in the morning light. You can see totally different things, objects and forms at that time. The lonely rails of the Western Bahnhof and the towers of that building together with the big mass of concrete really caught my eye.

The Exposure:
Camera: Nikon D200
Lens: F2.8
Post-production: Photoshop

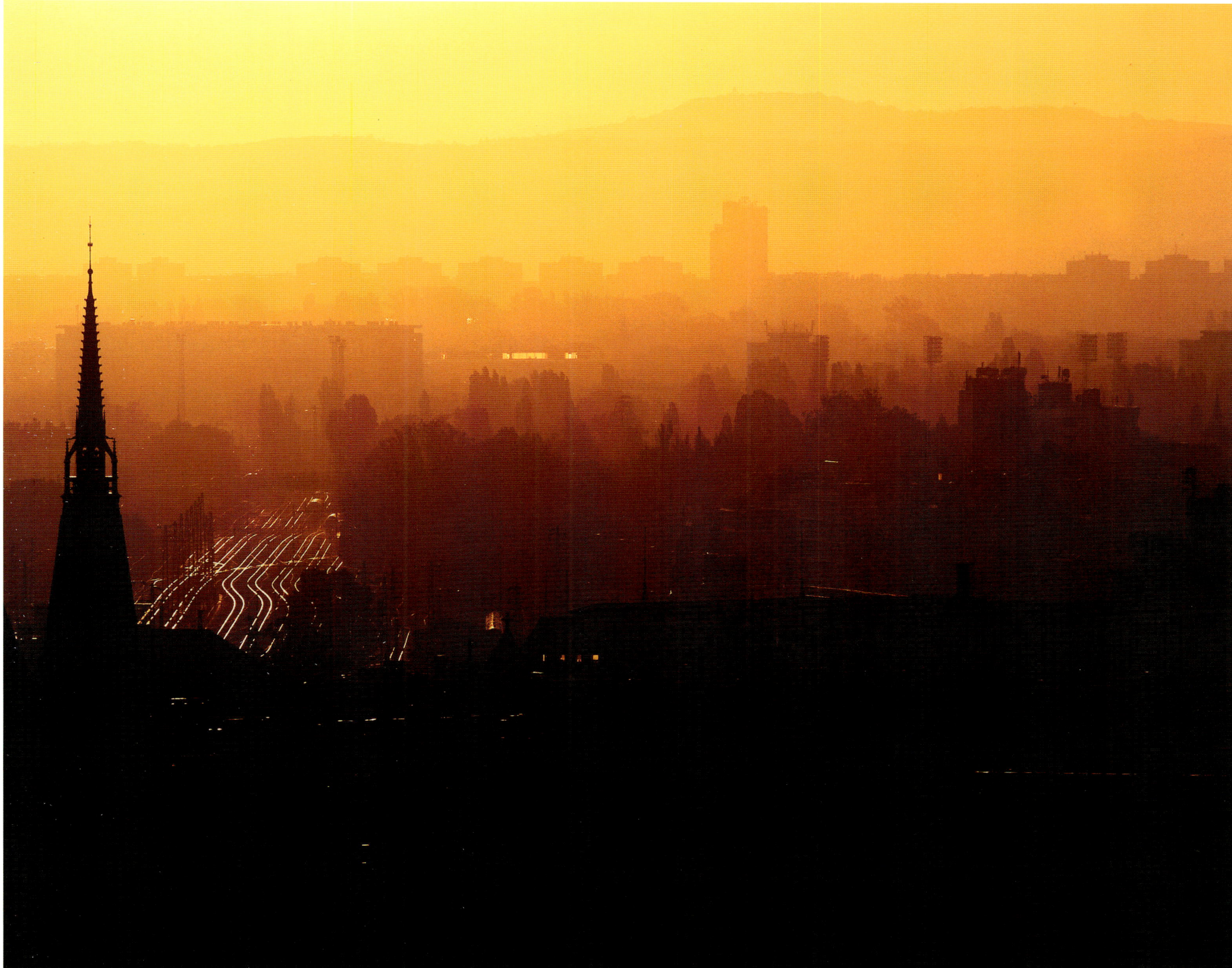

Name: Zoltán Balogh, 31
Nationality: Hungarian
Status: Professional
Photographer since: 2006
Favourite Camera of all Time:
Konica Minolta 7D
Influences: The people, the street, nature

The Location: Budapest, Hungary

The Story: This railway station is the main travel centre of the capital and it is always busy and crowded with people travelling all around the country. I was trying to capture a few minutes of down time in the morning hours before the big rush.

The Exposure:
Camera: Konica Minolta 7D
Lens: Minolta AF 17-35mm 2.8-4
Settings: F2.8 @ 1/20 sec ISO 800
Post-production: Photoshop

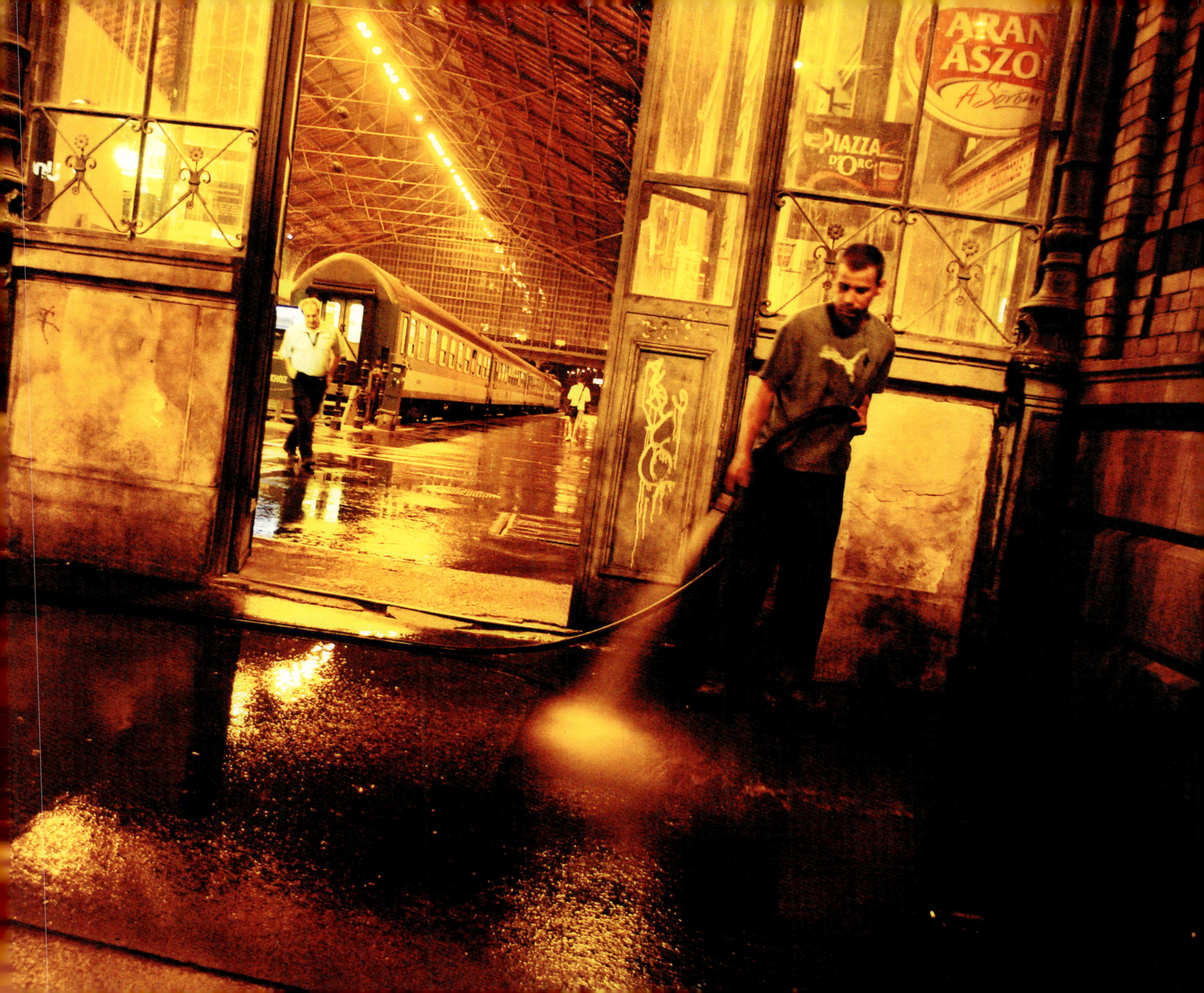
ARAN
ÁSZO
PIAZZA
D'OR

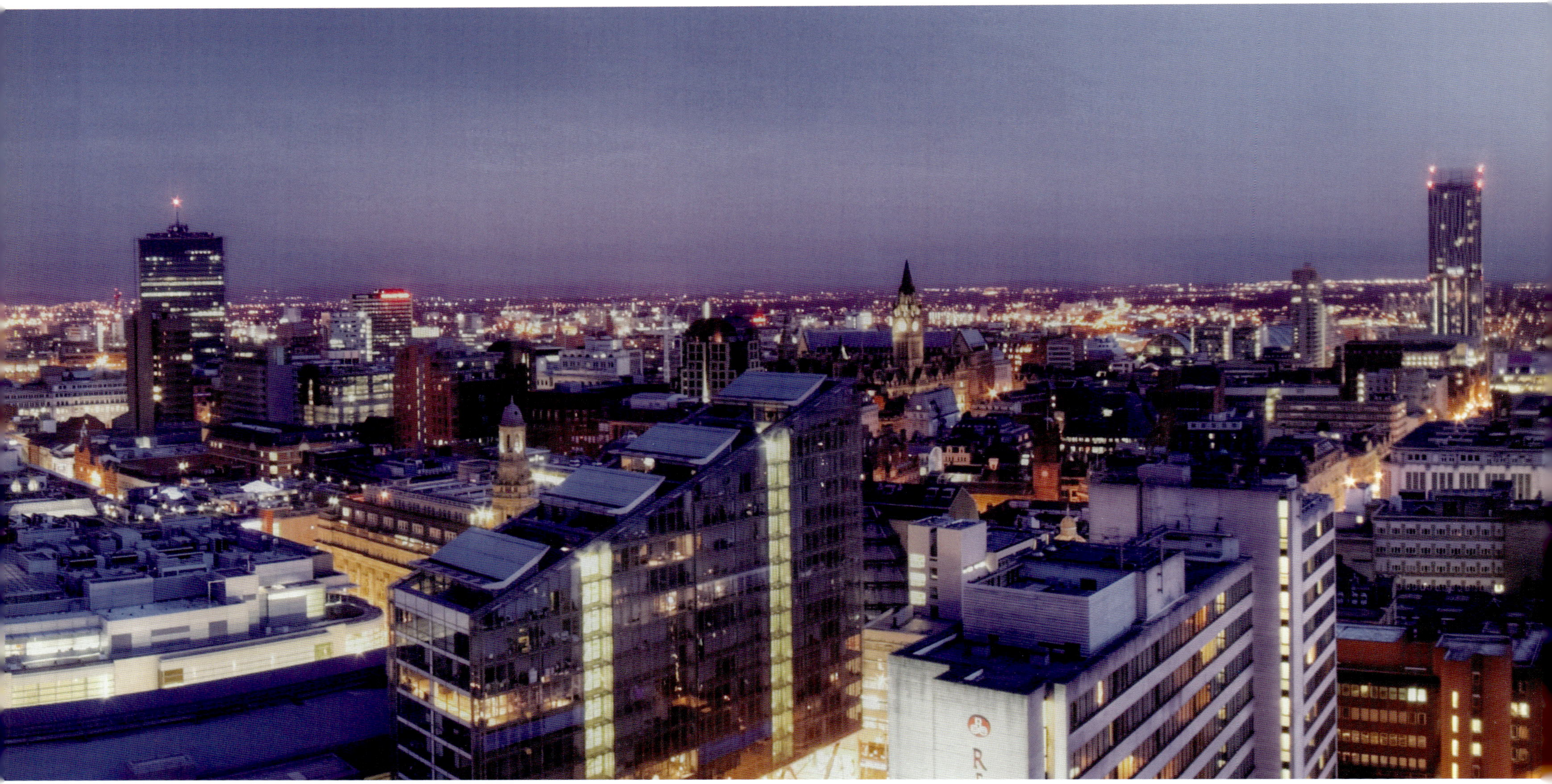

Name: Tom Sanderson, 30
Nationality: English
Status: Amateur
Photographer since: 1995
Favourite Camera of all Time:
Nikon D3x
Influences: Joe Cornish, Colin Prior, Matt Stuart

The Location: Manchester, UK

The Story: One clear night while out urbexing in Manchester, I noticed a rooftop that looked like it would be a good vantage point for a city landscape, so up we went and shot a few frames.

The Exposure:
Camera: Canon 350D
Lens: Sigma 10-20mm F/4-5.6
Settings: F11 @ 30 sec ISO 100
Post-production: Photoshop

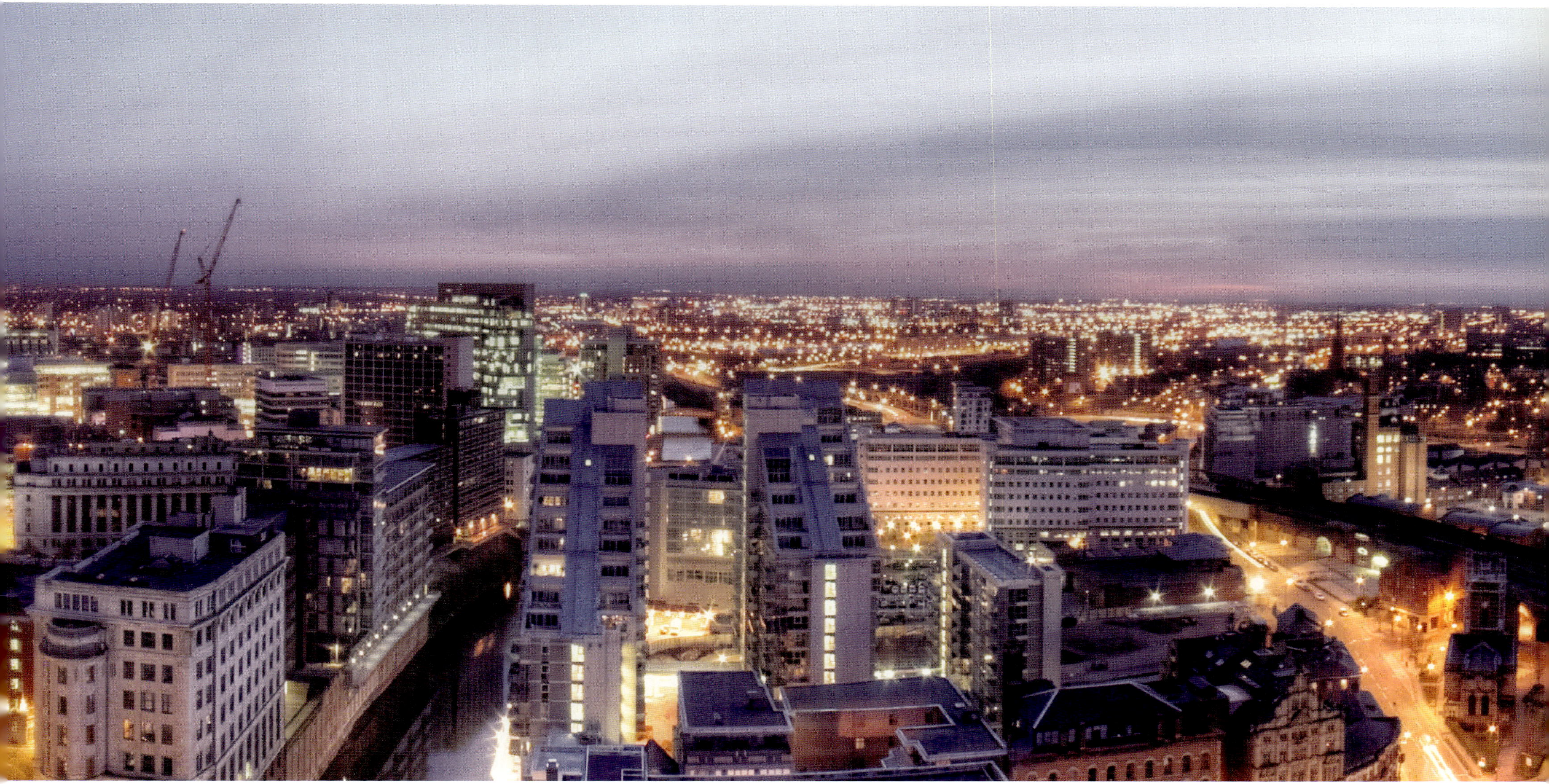

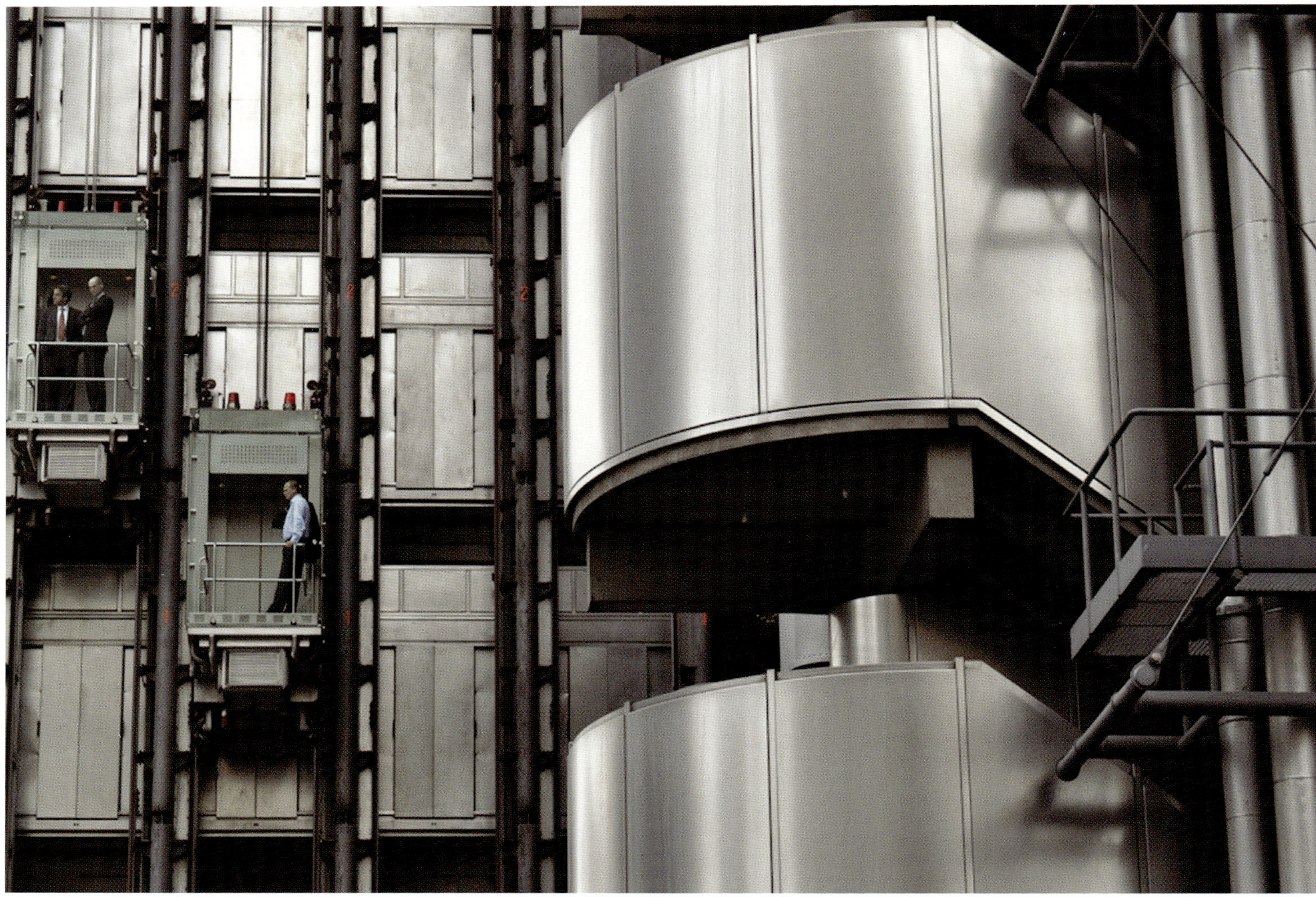

Name: James Murray, 40
Nationality: Scottish
Status: Student photographer
Photographer since: 1989
Favourite Camera of all Time:
Nikon F80
Influences: Herbet List, Alexandro Rodchenko, Keith Carter, Puressence

The Location: London, UK

The Story: I was fascinated with the size, scale and metal exterior of this particular building. The modernistic and industrial look is well complemented by the glass elevators. After a while of watching these elevators zip up and down I got to thinking it was like watching worker bees navigating the hive. Shooting from distance and waiting for a decisive moment was all that was required.

The Exposure:
Camera: Nikon D 90
Lens: Nikkor 55-200mm
Settings: F6.3 @ 1/200sec ISO 500
Post-production: Photoshop

Name: Santiago Urquijo, 45
Nationality: Spain
Status: Amateur
Photographer since: 1980
Favourite Camera of all Time:
Canon 5D mark II
Influences: Steve McCurry, Galen Rowell, Sebastiao Salgado

The Location: Fez-el-Bali, Morocco

The Story: I got up very early to try to capture the medina in another light and see it without anyone on it. No sooner had I arrived that this poultry merchant appeared out of the blue.

The Exposure:
Camera: Canon 350d
Lens: Sigma 17-70mm F2.8-4.5
Settings: F5 @ 1/100 sec ISO 100
Post-production: Lightroom

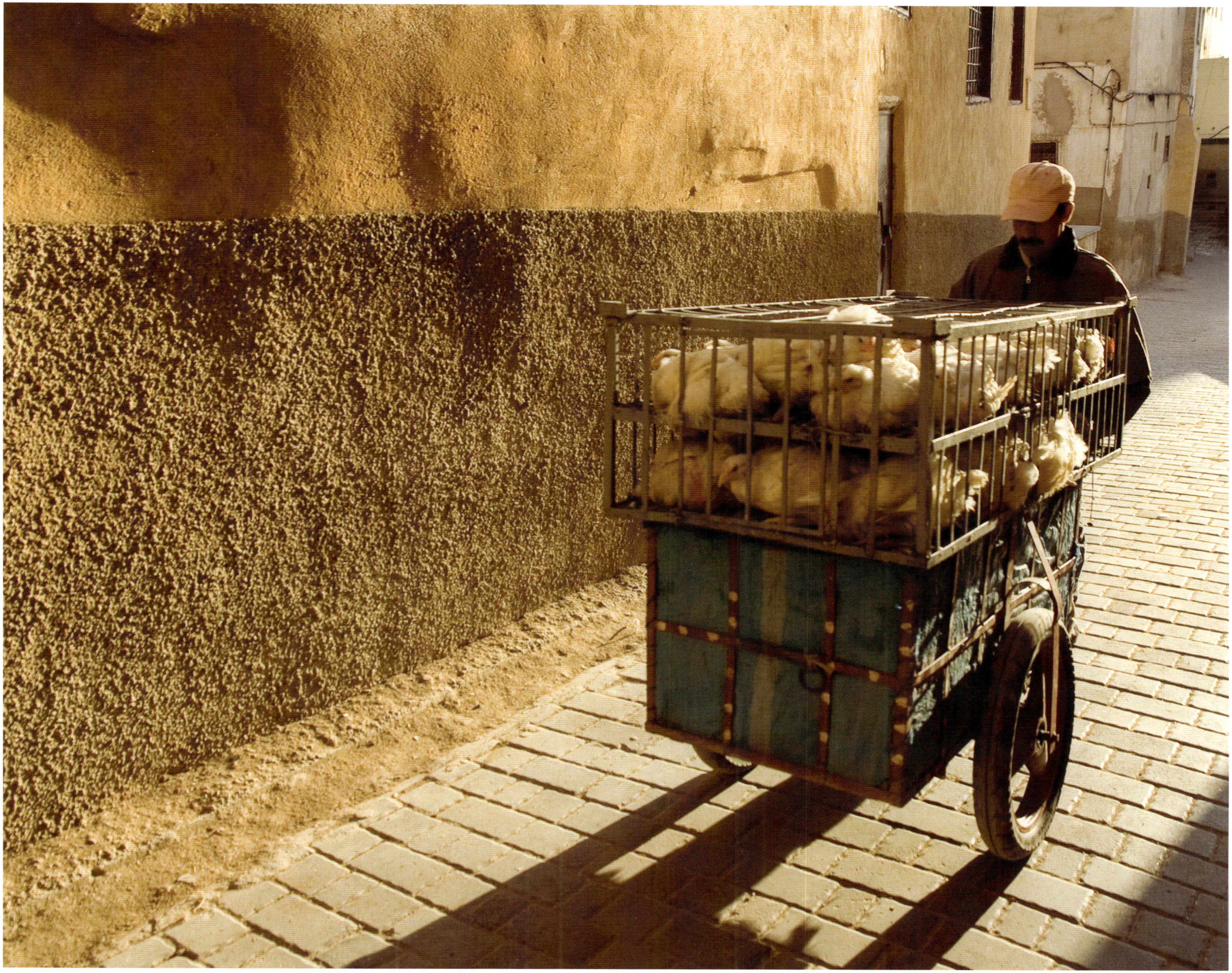

Name: Paul Swinney, 25
Nationality: English
Status: Amateur
Photographer since: 2007
Favourite Camera of all Time: Nikon D3x
Influences: Stuart Clarke

The Location: Cambridge, UK

The Story: We were coming back from Trinity College's annual May Ball. After a hard year of studying, the students of Cambridge University celebrate the end of exams in what is known as May Week (which is actually in June). As the sun rose on a new day, I held back from my group of friends to capture them walking back home from the ball as the rest of the city awoke.

The Exposure:
Camera: Nikon Coolpix 775
Settings: F7.9 @ ISO100
Post-production: Photoshop

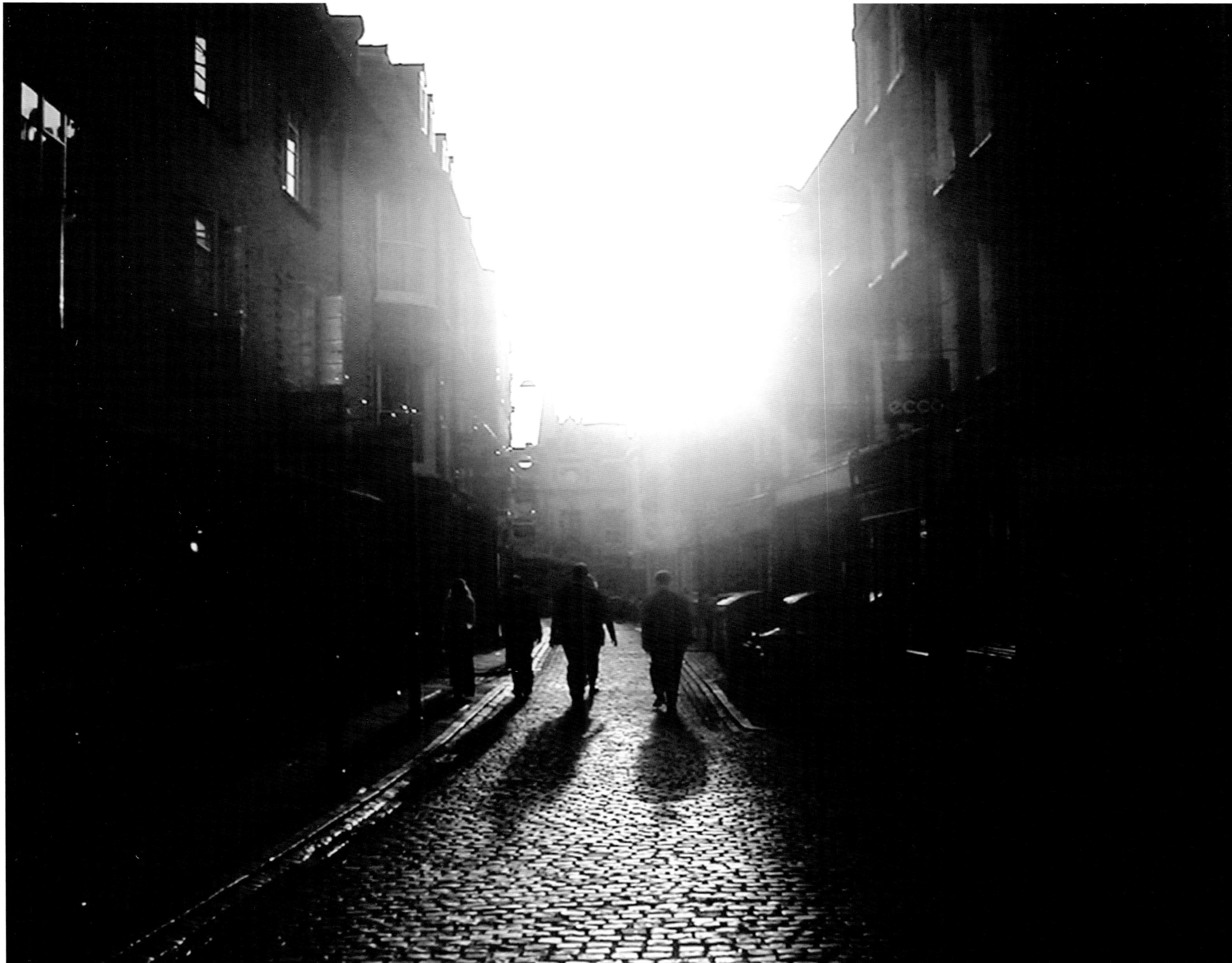

Name: Dean Yeadon, 44
Nationality: South African
Status: Amateur
Photographer since: 1990
Favourite Camera of all Time:
Hasselblad H3d
Influences: Steve McCurry

The Location: Mont Lubin, Rodrigues Island, Mauritius

The Story: The symmetry of the same clothing patterns of the mother and child awaiting a haircut immediately caught my attention.

The Exposure:
Camera: Hasselblad H3D
Lens: F11
Settings: F8 @ 1/45 sec ISO 100
Post-production: Aperture

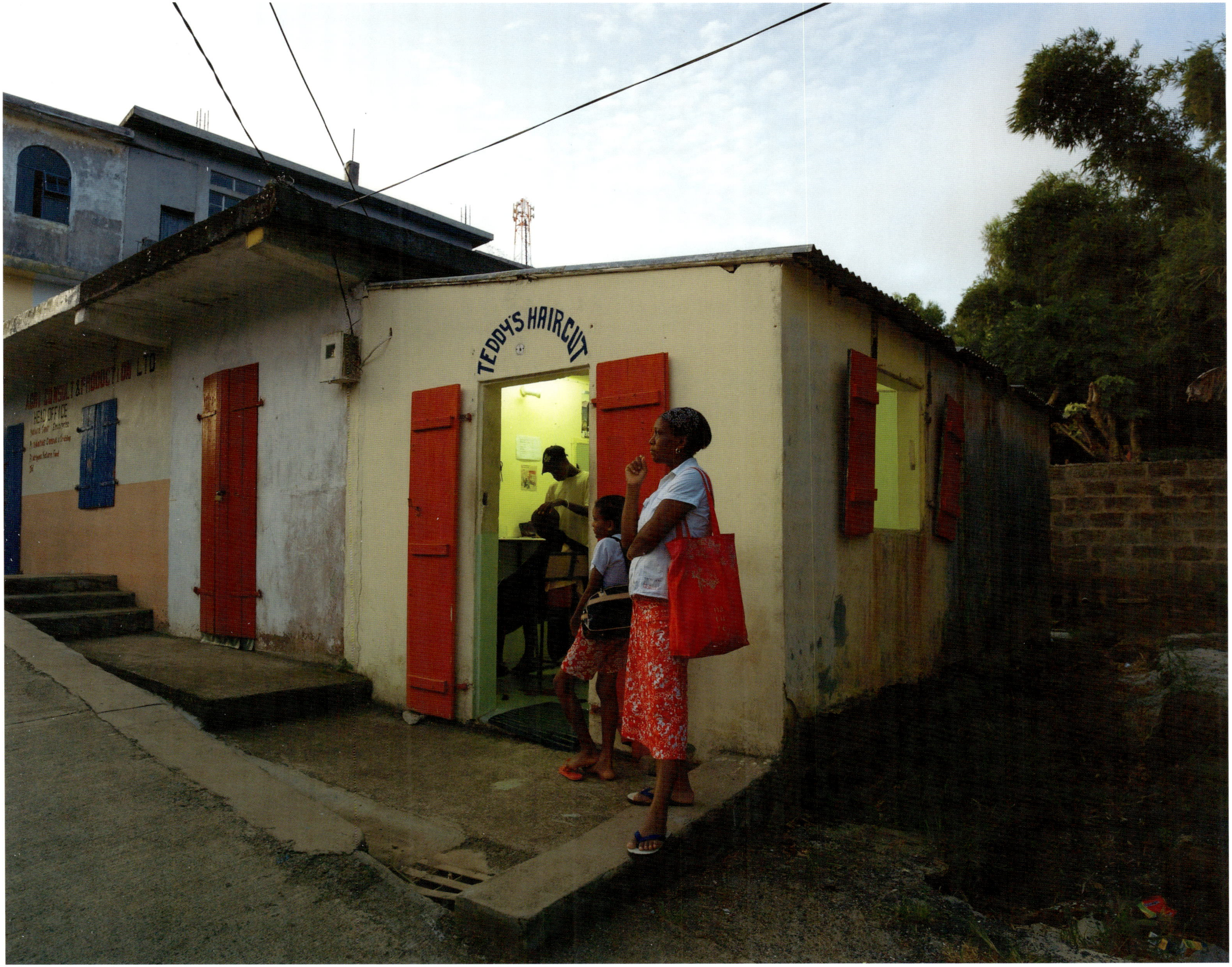
TEDDY'S HAIRCUT
& PRODUCTION LTD
HEAD OFFICE

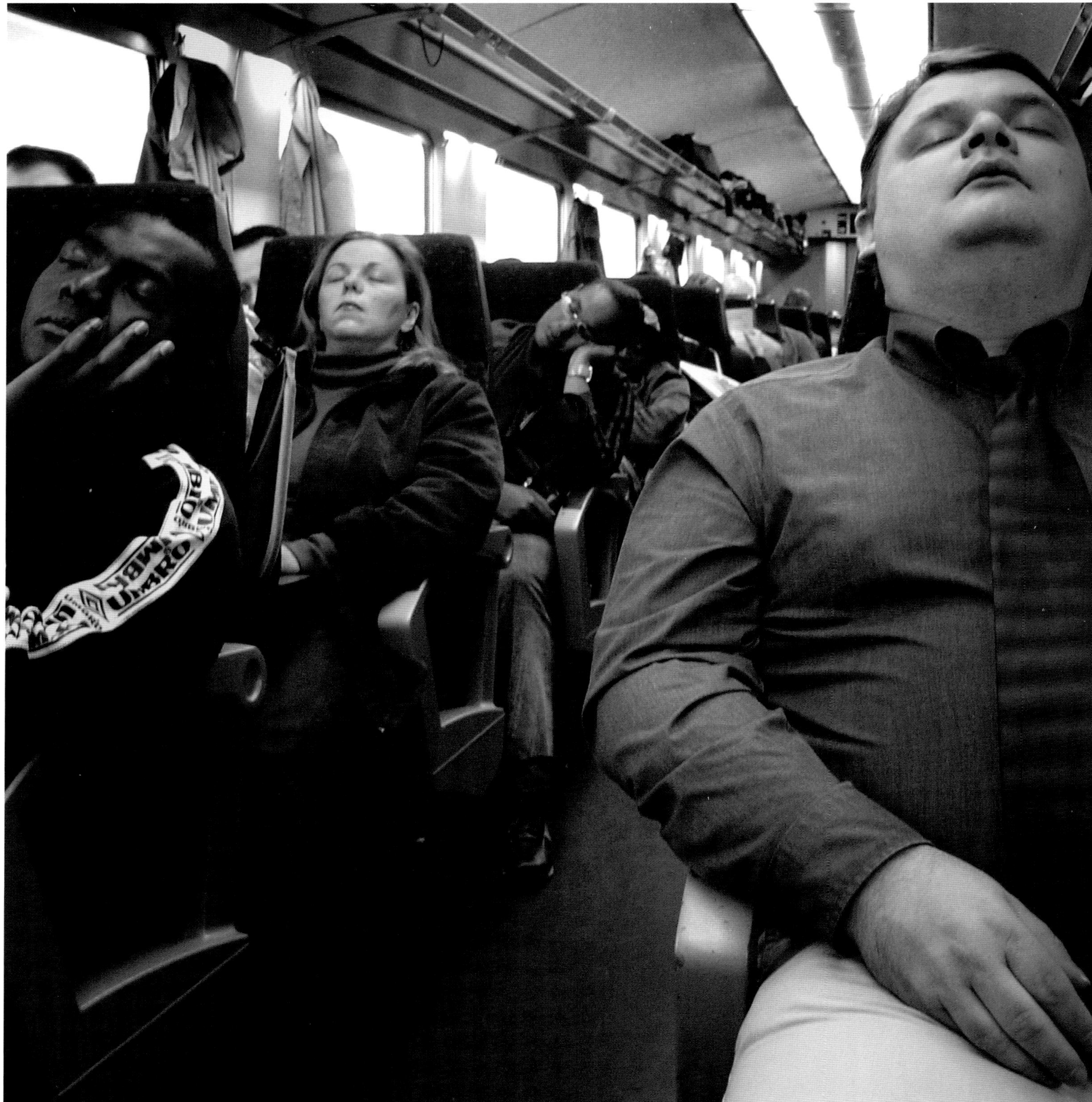

Name: Anaiz iTo , 37
Nationality: Belgian
Status: Amateur
Photographer since: 2009
Favourite Camera of all Time:
Canon 5D Mark II
Influences: Life, dreams and nightmares!

The Location: Train Liège-Bruxelles, Belgium

The Story: To get work, people have to travel out of town to Brussels because there is no work here in my town Liège. So they slip into a second life that fills the long journey to work and back each day. It starts so early and finishes so late. Everyone is tired.

The Exposure:
Camera: Sony DSC-V1
Post-production: Photoshop

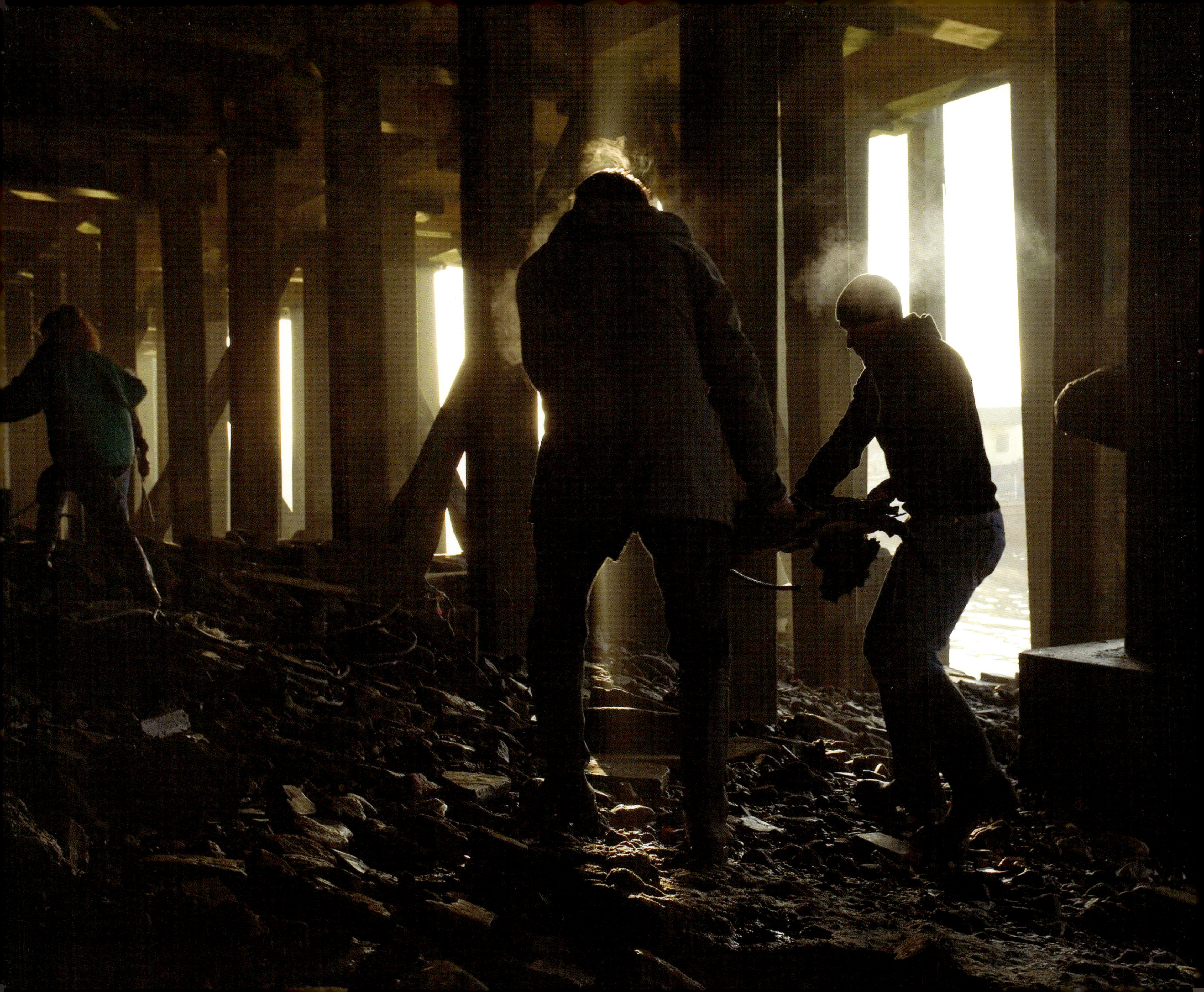

Name: Anthony Epes, 43
Nationality: American
Status: Professional
Photographer since: 1999
Favourite Camera of all Time:
Hasselblad 503 cx
Influences: Ernst Haas, Ansel Adams, H.C Bresson

The Location: London, UK

The Story: I had been creating a series of early morning light studies along the Thames for an exhibition. I stumbled across these workmen right down at ground level where most people never go. The silhouettes created by the dawn light just accentuated the hard manual labour it takes to maintain the banks of the river.

The Exposure:
Camera: Canon 5D
Lens: F4L 17-40mm
Post-production: Lightroom

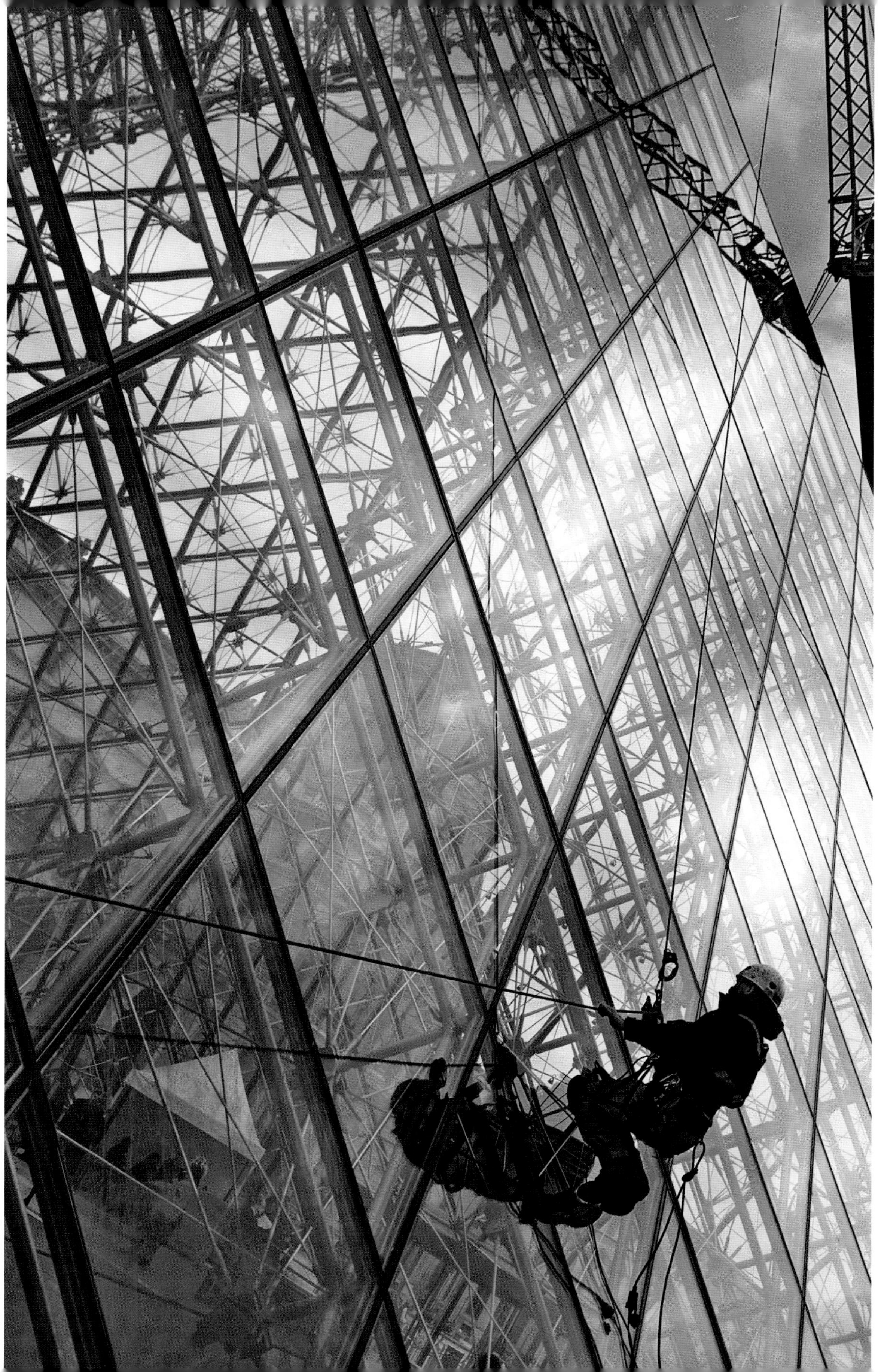

Name: Andrey Belyakov, 44
Nationality: Ukrainian
Status: Amateur
Photographer since: 2000
Favourite Camera of all Time:
EOS5D Mark II
Influences: Streets, People

The Location: Paris, France

The Story: I was just walking with my family near the Louvre Museum, and, suddenly, I saw two guys who were bravely and carefully cleaning windows on the Louvre Pyramid which is a large glass and metal pyramid. As they rose on the elevating crane, I captured the image from the lower angle.

The Exposure:
Camera: Canon EOS5D Mark II
Lens: Canon EF28-135mm f/3.5-5.6 IS USM
Settings: F/4.2
Post-production: Photoshop

Name: Jean-Luc Rollier, 63
Nationality: French
Status: Amateur
Photographer since: 1970
Favourite Camera of all Time: Nikon F2
Influences: Robert Frank, Robert Doisneau, HCB, Elliot Erwitt

The Location: Berlin, Germany

The Story: In Berlin, the bicycle is a popular way to go around town. There are a lot of cycling lanes and pedestrians have to be very aware and careful as the cyclists go fast! I took this picture very quickly, turning backwards, after I was nearly hit by this musician in a rush.

The Exposure:
Camera: Nikon D80
Lens: 200 mm
Settings: F5,6/ 1/500e sec ISO 400
Post-production: Irfanview

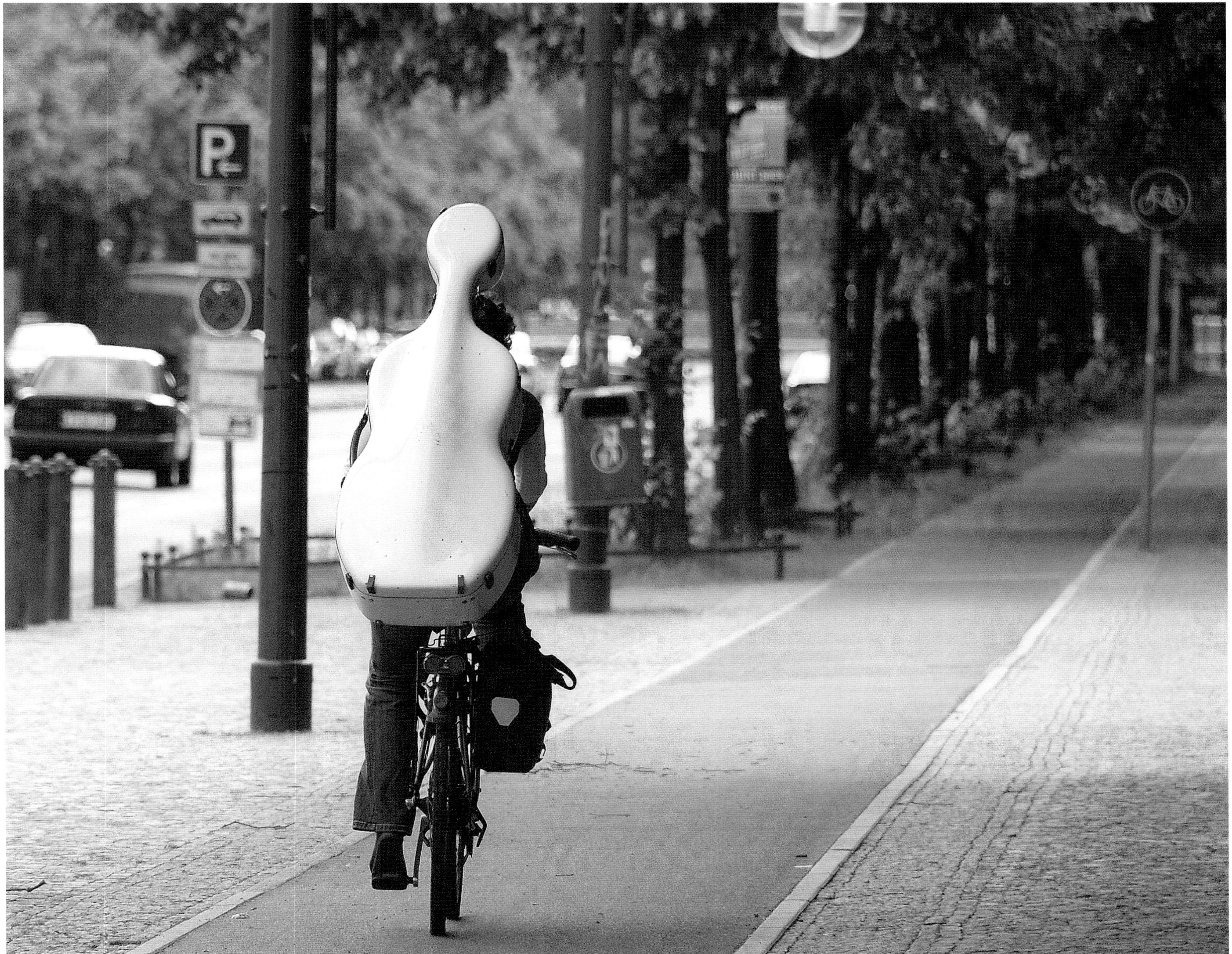

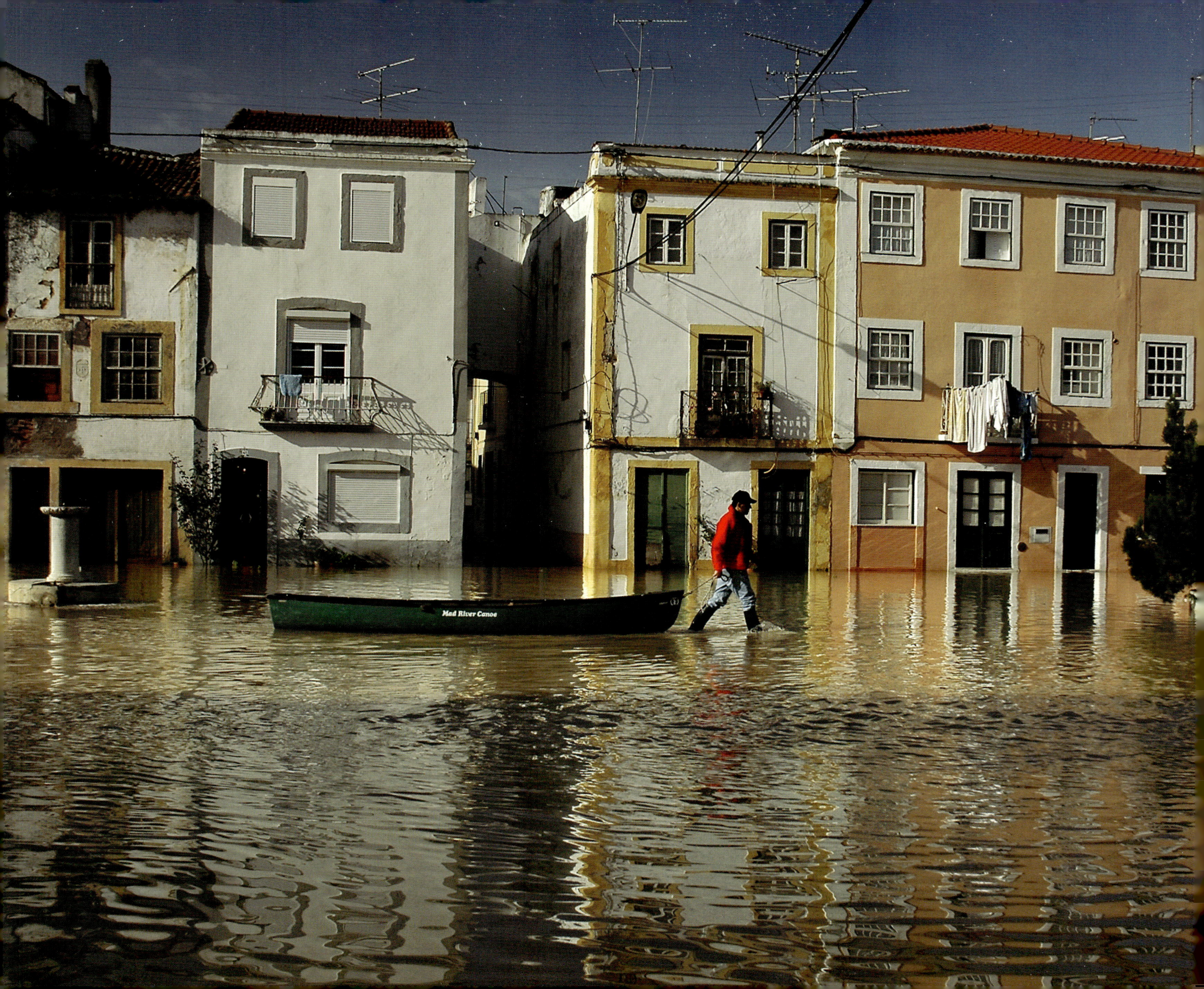
Mad River Canoe

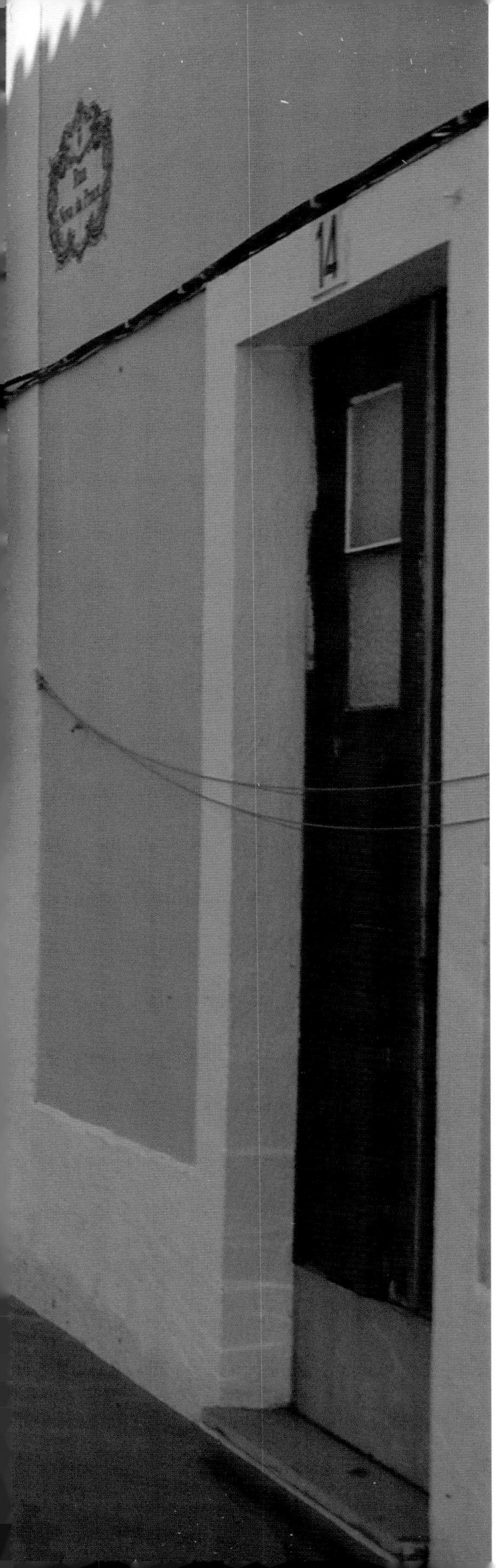

Name: Ana Filipa Scarpa, 51
Nationality: Portuguese
Status: Amateur
Photographer since: 2005
Favourite Camera of all Time: Nikon D3
Influences: Ansell Adams, Erik Almas, Andy Biggs, Ralph Gibson

The Location: Santarém, Portugal

The Story: The locals of the village had been warned that the river would climb the bank and that the floods were expected during the night. Everyone was on alert and they found alternative ways of coping.

The Exposure:
Camera: Nikon D70
Lens: Nikon Nikkor AF-S DX 18-70mm F/3.5-4.5G IF ED
Settings: F8 @ 1/250 sec ISO 200
Post-production: Photoshop, Lightroom, Nik Sharpener

Name: Mihály Kondella, 27
Nationality: Hungarian
Status: Semi-Professional
Photographer since: 2001
Favourite Camera of all Time:
Canon 5D Mark II
Influences: Joe Buissink, Robert Capa

The Location: Helsinki, Finland

The Story: My favourite city of all time is Helsinki. One morning we went to explore an area we hadn't yet been. We arrived at this Flea Market where different nationalities and groups of people try to sell and buy various items.

The Exposure:
Camera: Nikon D200
Lens: Nikkor AF-S 17-55/2.8
Settings: F2.8 @ 1/25 sec ISO 640
Post-production: Photoshop

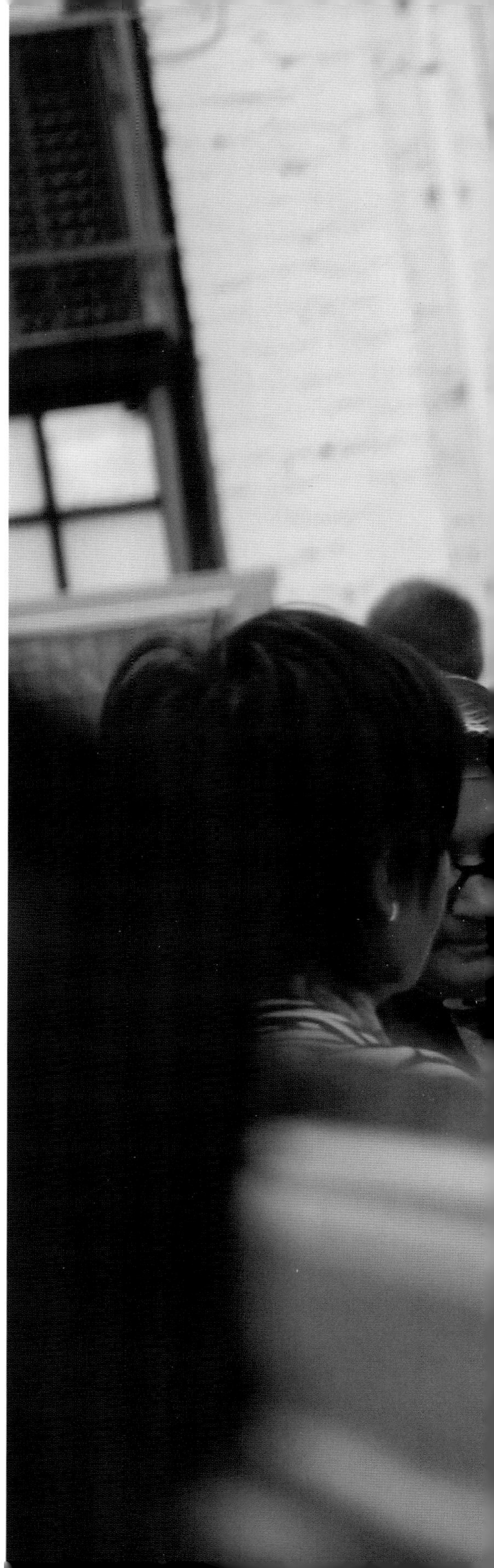

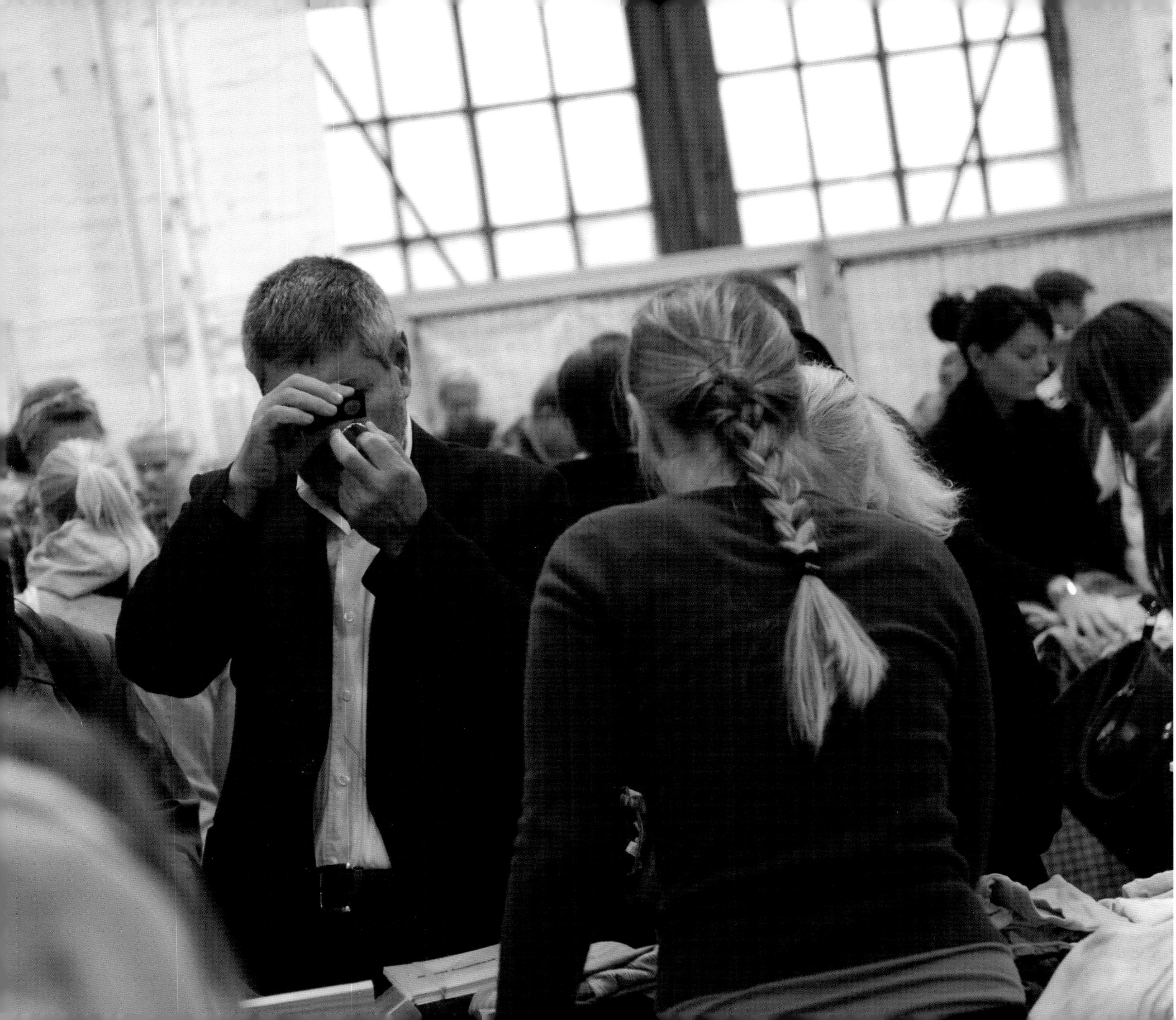

Name: Jovan Gojković, 24
Nationality: Serbian
Status: Amateur
Photographer since: 2007
Favourite Camera of all Time:
Canon 5D Mark II
Influences: Henri Cartier-Bresson,
Robert Capa, James Nachtwey

The Location: Niš, Serbia

The Story: People in this photo are workers at a recycling center in the industrial zone of city of Niš, Serbia. They are collecting scrap metal everyday for minimum wage. This photo is dedicated to all the hard workers and it is a story about survival in this consumer society.

The Exposure:
Camera: Canon EOS 30D
Lens: Canon 18-55mm, F3.5-5.6
Settings: F5.6 @ 1/160 sec ISO 200
Post-production: Photoshop CS3, Nick Software Silver Efex Pro

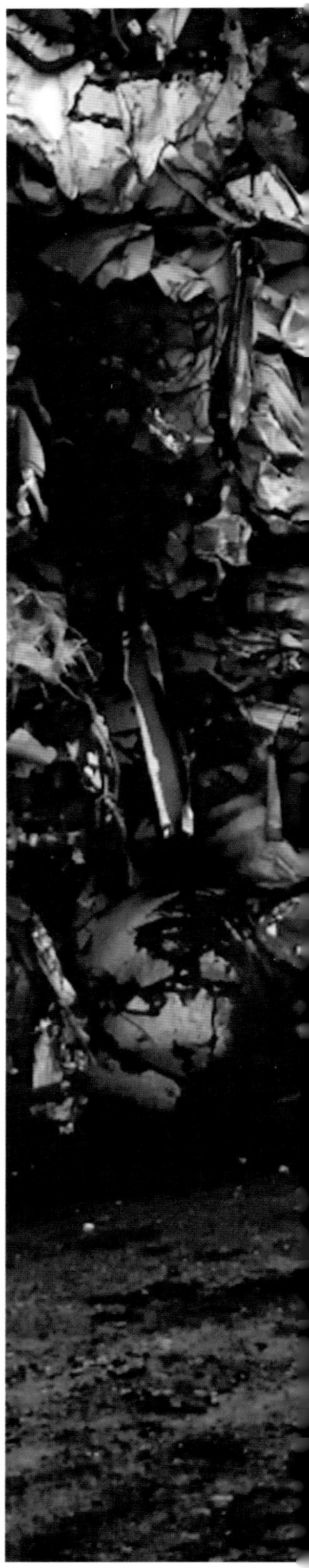

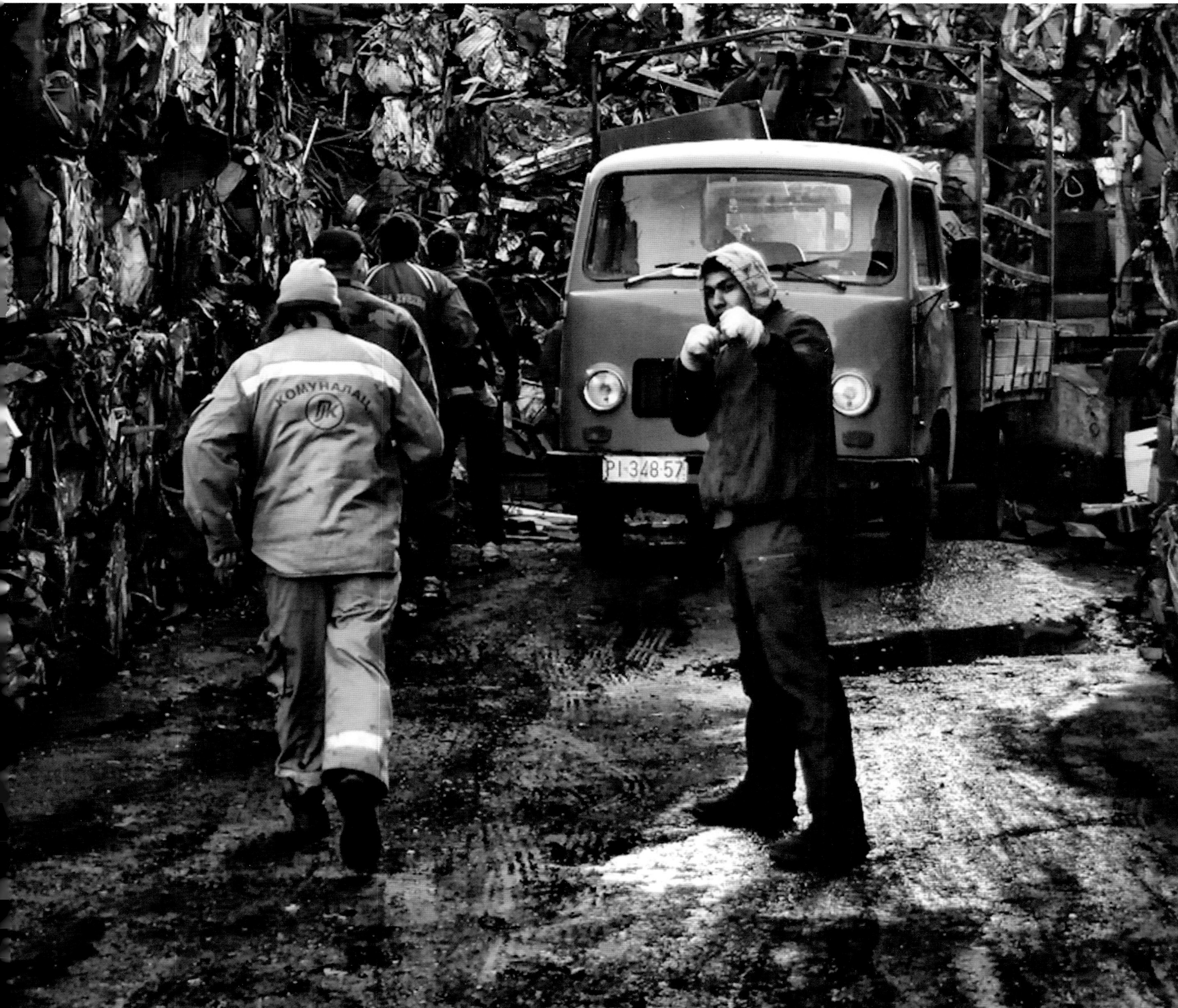
КОМУНАЛАЦ
PI·348·57

Name: Armen A. Dolukhanyan, 39
Nationality: Armenian
Status: Amateur
Photographer since: 1988
Favourite Camera of all Time:
Voigtlander Bessa
Influences: Henri Cartier-Bresson,
Garik Avanesian

The Location: Kharkov, Ukraine

The Story: From far away I saw a girl, walking towards me. I decided to take a picture of her. I focused on the foreground and when she entered the frame I pressed the button. I liked that three figures in the background seem like one, three unfamiliar solitudes, united in this frame. This only can happen in street photography.

The Exposure:
Camera: Voigtlander Bessa-R3a
Lens: Voigtlander Nokton 40mm f/1.4
Settings: F5.6 @ 1/250 sec Ilford XP-2 Film
Post-production: Photoshop

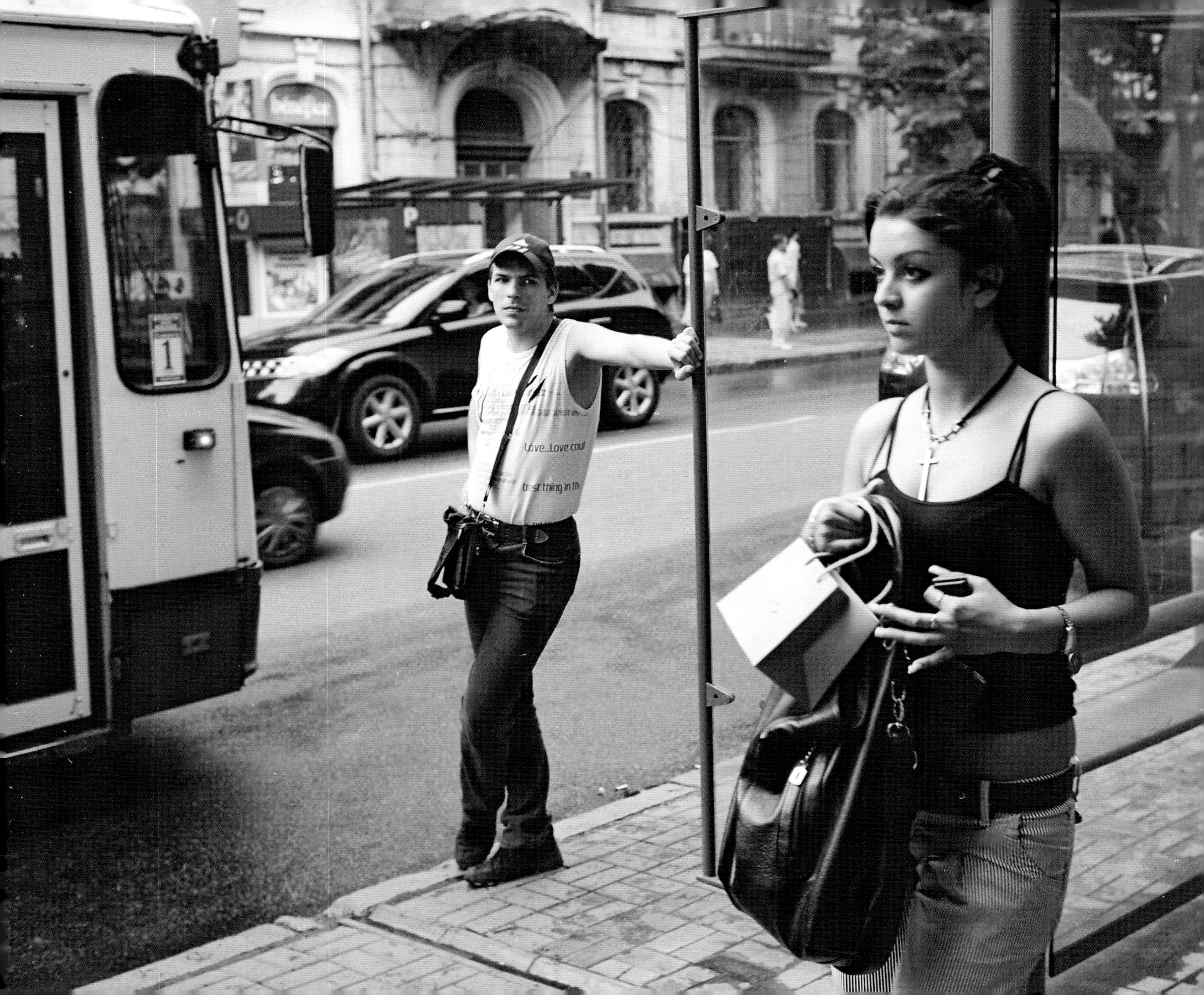
1
P
Love...Love coul
best thing in th

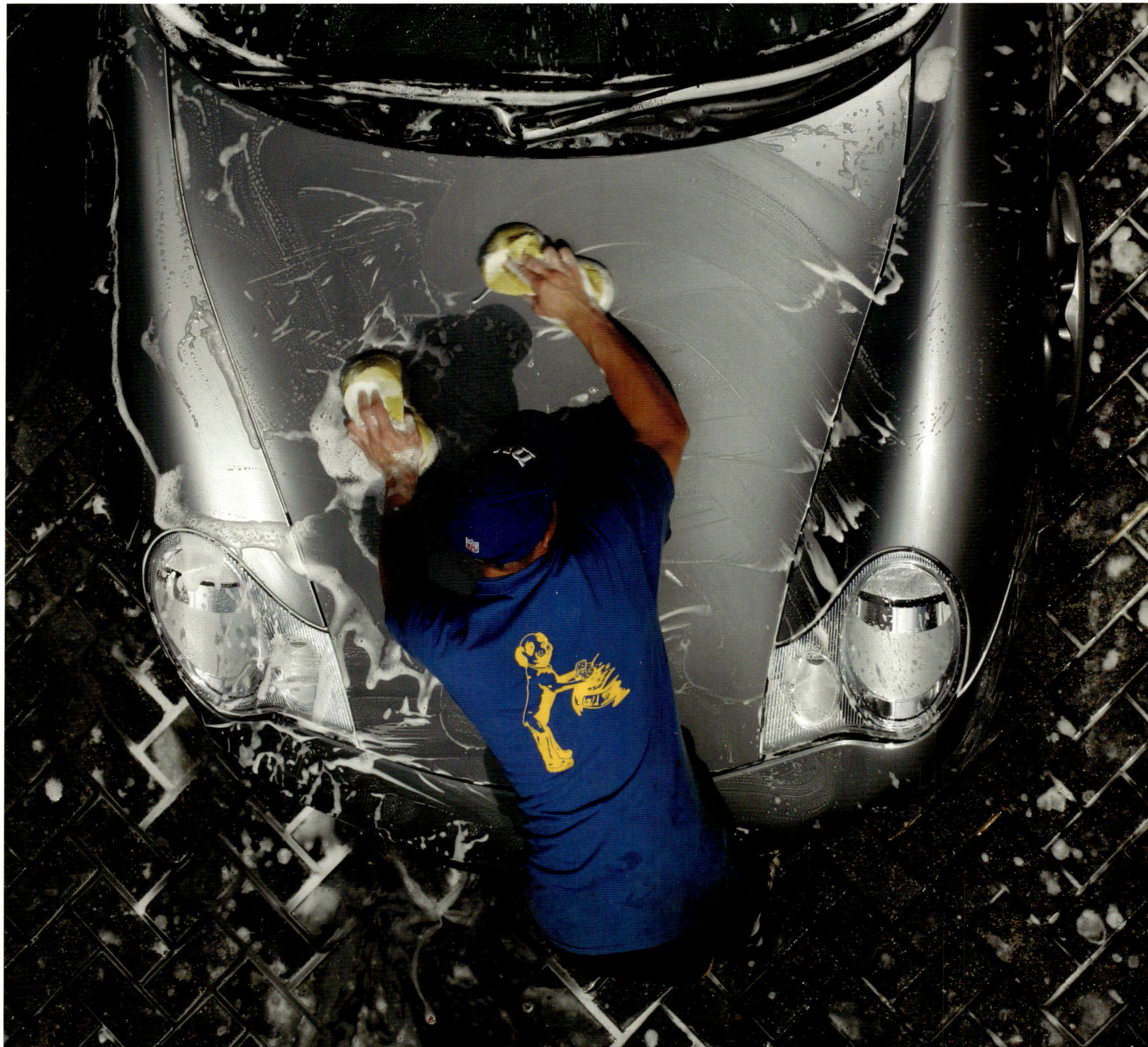

Name: Chris Mole, 50
Nationality: UK
Status: Amateur
Photographer since: 1976
Favourite Camera of all Time: Canon 7D
Influences: Martin Parr

The Location: Brighton Marina, UK

The Story: I was in a multi-storey car park overlooking a car cleaning business and was drawn by the unusual perspective and different patterns and lines.

The Exposure:
Camera: Canon 20D
Lens: 90mm
Settings: F9 @ 1/400 sec ISO 100
Post-production: Photoshop levels and cropping

Name: Reza Golchin, 32
Nationality: Iranian
Status: Professional
Photographer since: 2000
Favourite Camera of all Time: Canon 5D
Influences: Ed Weston, my brother

The Location: Khorramabad, Iran

The Story: This photo is from the Ashoura mourning ritual held in the town of Korramabad in Lorestan, Province of Iran located in the western part of the country. In the town of Korramabad, women in black Chador light candles in 40 stations on the day preceding Ashoura. They cover their face with a piece of cloth and re-enact the carvan which mourned the martyrdom of Imam Husayn. The Mourning of Muharram is an important period of mourning in the Shi'a branch of Islam, taking place in Muharram, the first month of the Islamic calendar. It is also called the Remembrance of Muharram.

The Exposure:
Camera: Canon 5D
Lens: F3.5-5.6
Settings: F5 @ 1/60 sec ISO 400
Post-production: Photoshop

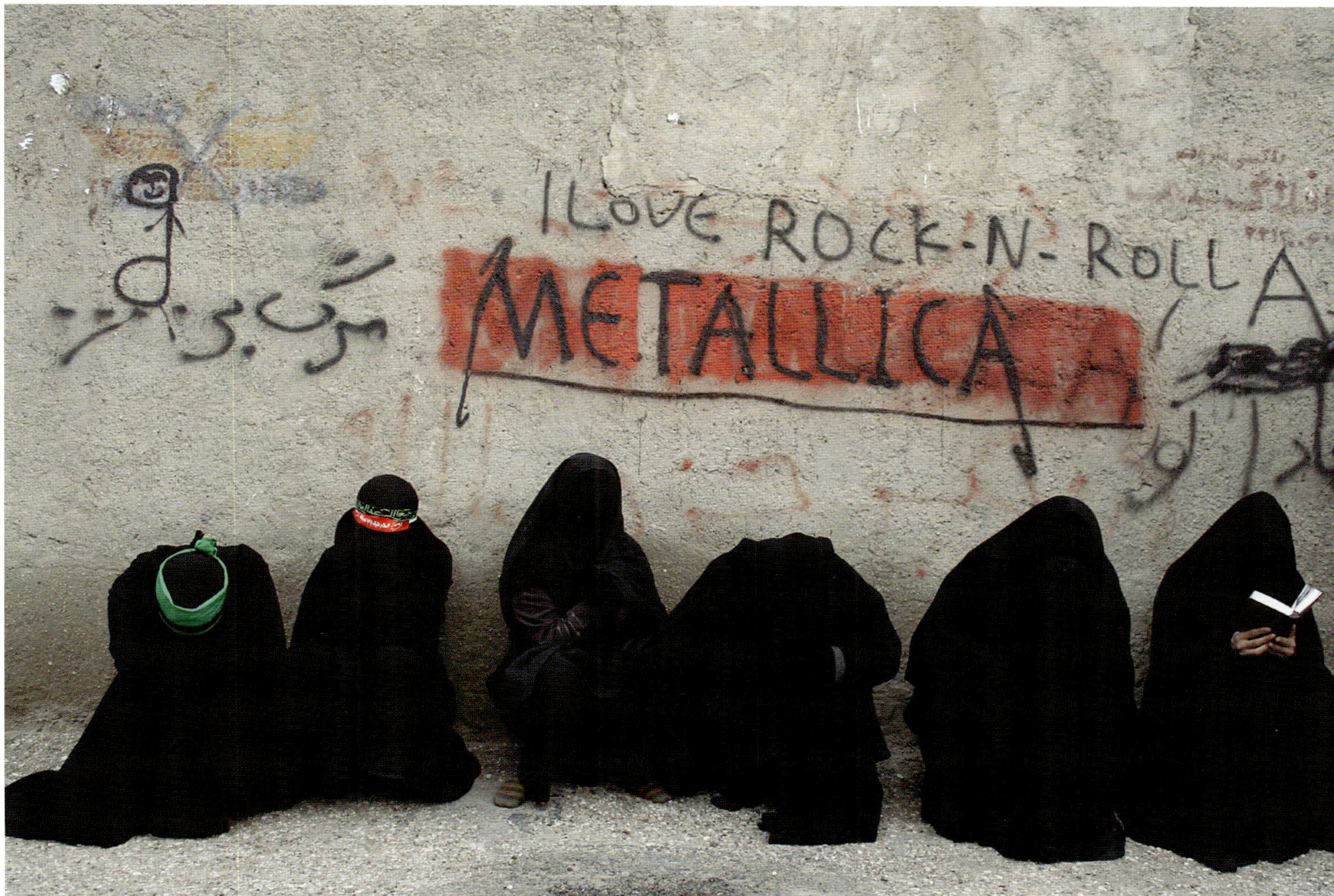
I LOVE ROCK-N-ROLL
METALLICA

Name: Ian Monk, 52
Nationality: British
Status: Amateur
Photographer since: 2007
Favourite Camera of all Time: Leica M9
Influences: Nadav Kander

The Location: Prague, Czech Republic

The Story: The whole area around Prague Castle lends itself to street photography. For me what sets this particular scene apart is the diagonal shaft of light illuminating the smoke and the expression of the blacksmith.

The Exposure:
Camera: Nikon D90
Lens: Nikkor 18-105 f/3.5-5.6G ED VR
Settings: F4.5 @ 1/320 sec ISO 200
Post-production: Capture NX2, Nik software Color Efex Pro

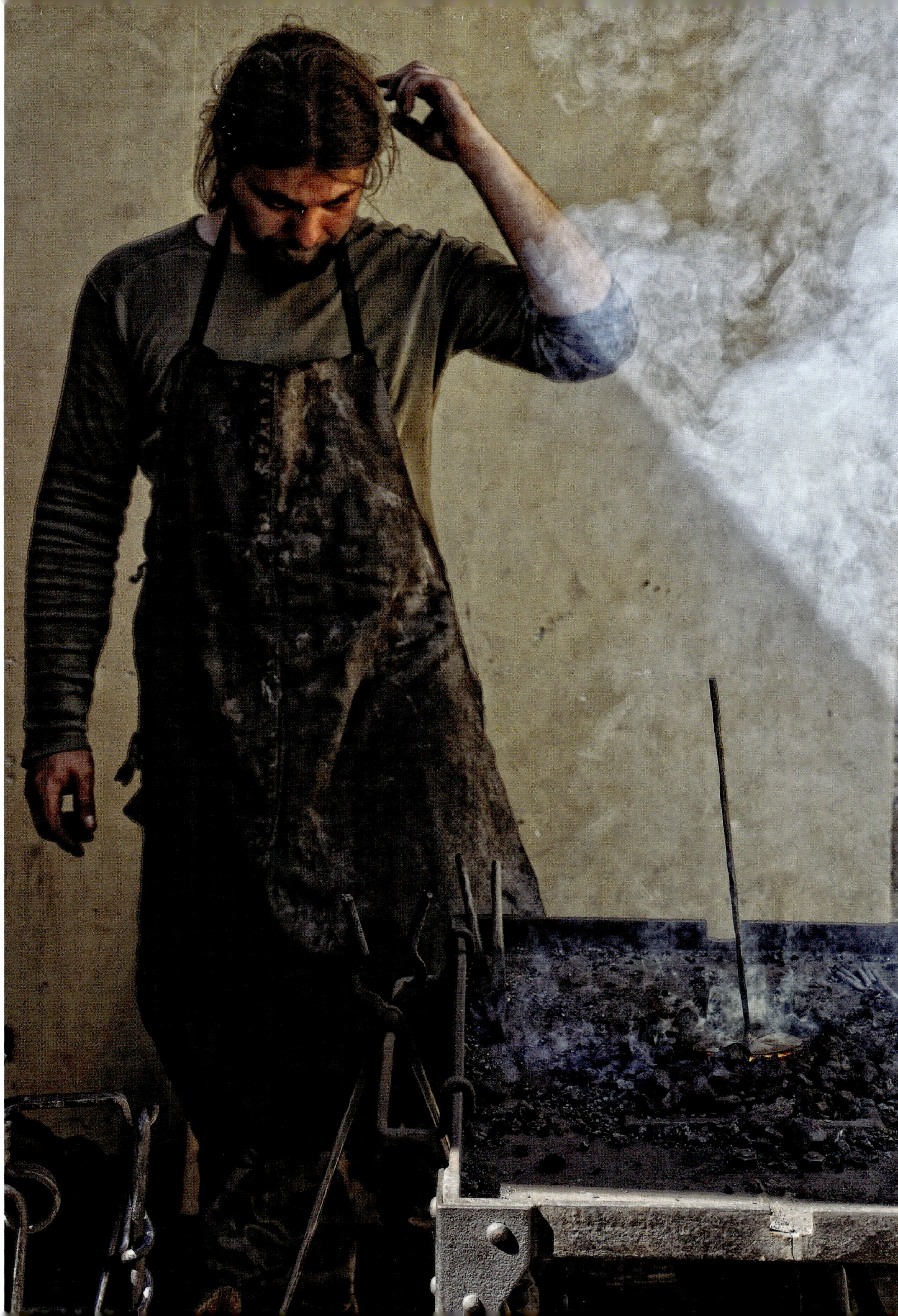

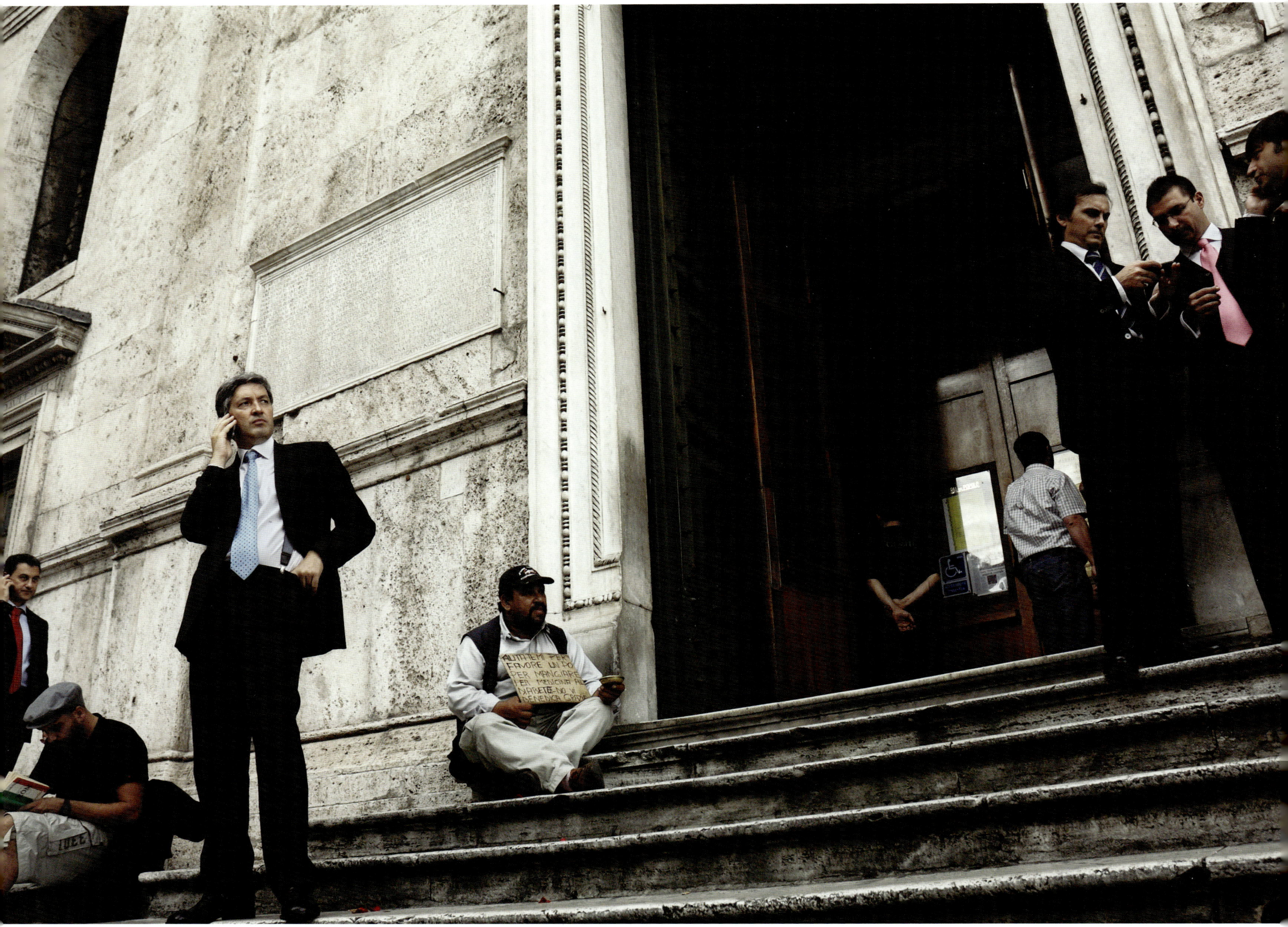
AIUTATEMI PER
FAVORE UN PO
PER MANGIARE
PER MEDICINA

Name: James Mortram, 39
Nationality: English
Status: Semi-professional
Photographer since: 2005
Favourite Camera of all Time: Nikon F
Influences: Tim Page, Don McCullin, Brian Lanker, W. Eugene Smith

The Location: Rome, Italy

The Story: It struck me I had stumbled upon a collision between; faith, money, style, despair and poverty outside a church adjacent to Piazza del Popolo.

The Exposure:
Camera: Nikon D200
Lens: 18 - 70mm F3.5 - f4.5 AF
Settings: F/6 ISO 320 18mm spot metered
Post-production: Photoshop

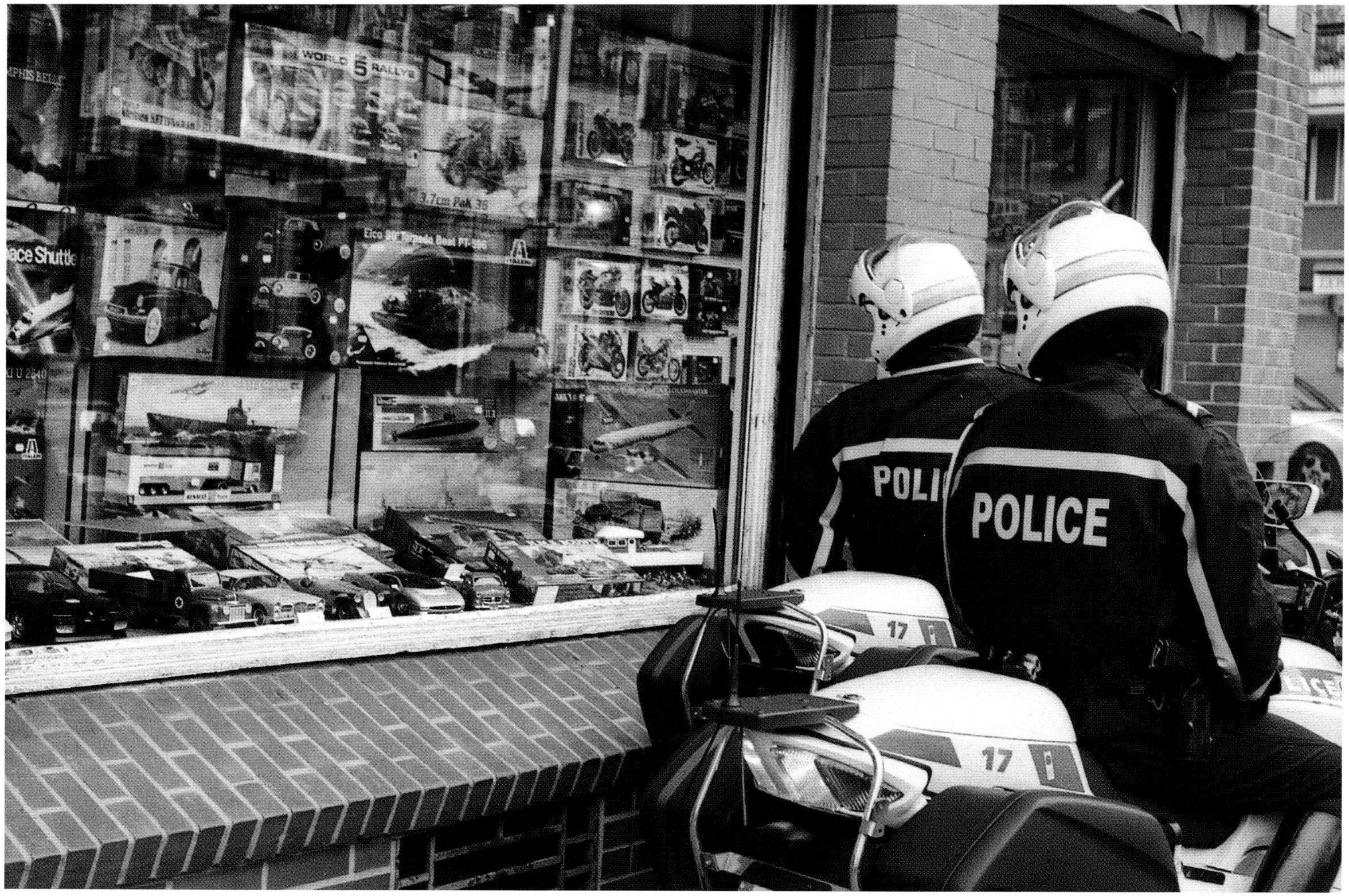
WORLD
5
RALLYS
POLICE
17

Name: Nathanaël Fournier, 29
Nationality: French
Photographer since: 2003
Favourite Camera of all Time: Leica M6
Influences: Abbas, Boubat, Cartier-Bresson, Riboud, Saul Leiter

The Location: Lille, France

The Story: There was a bomb alert in the centre of Lille. The police were on their way to clear the town and make the area safe. It just struck me that the line between adult and child, serious and frivolous is always blurred. It did not reflect on their competence.

The Exposure:
Camera: Praktika BC1
Lens: 50mm
Post-production: EpsonScan, Photoshop

Name: Mark Churly, 34
Nationality: English
Status: Amateur
Photographer since: 2009
Favourite Camera of all Time:
Fuji Finepix X100
Influences: William Eggleston, Henri Cartier Bresson

The Location: London, UK

The Story: I spotted these two men on top of the roof of the winter garden in Canary Wharf whilst I was getting myself a coffee at my work, on a cold January afternoon. I had my camera with me because I was in the midst of a year long photo a day project. I was able to capture a moment that mostly goes unnoticed, one that for me at least was a little reminiscent of some of those images I have seen of workers on New York skyscrapers from the 1930's.

The Exposure:
Camera: Canon Powershot S90
Settings: F/2 @ 1/500 sec ISO 80
Post-production: Aperture, Nik Silver Efex Pro

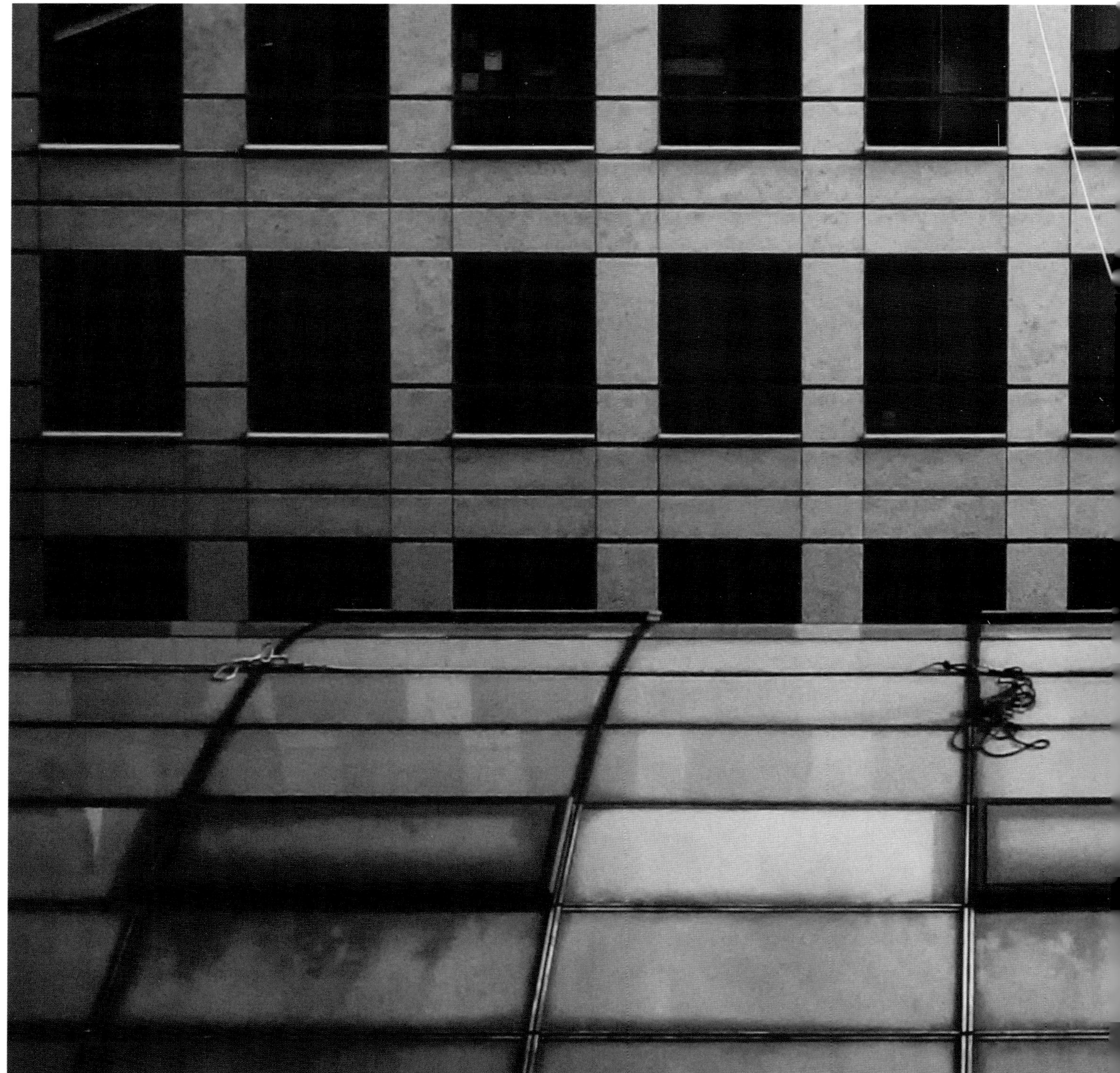

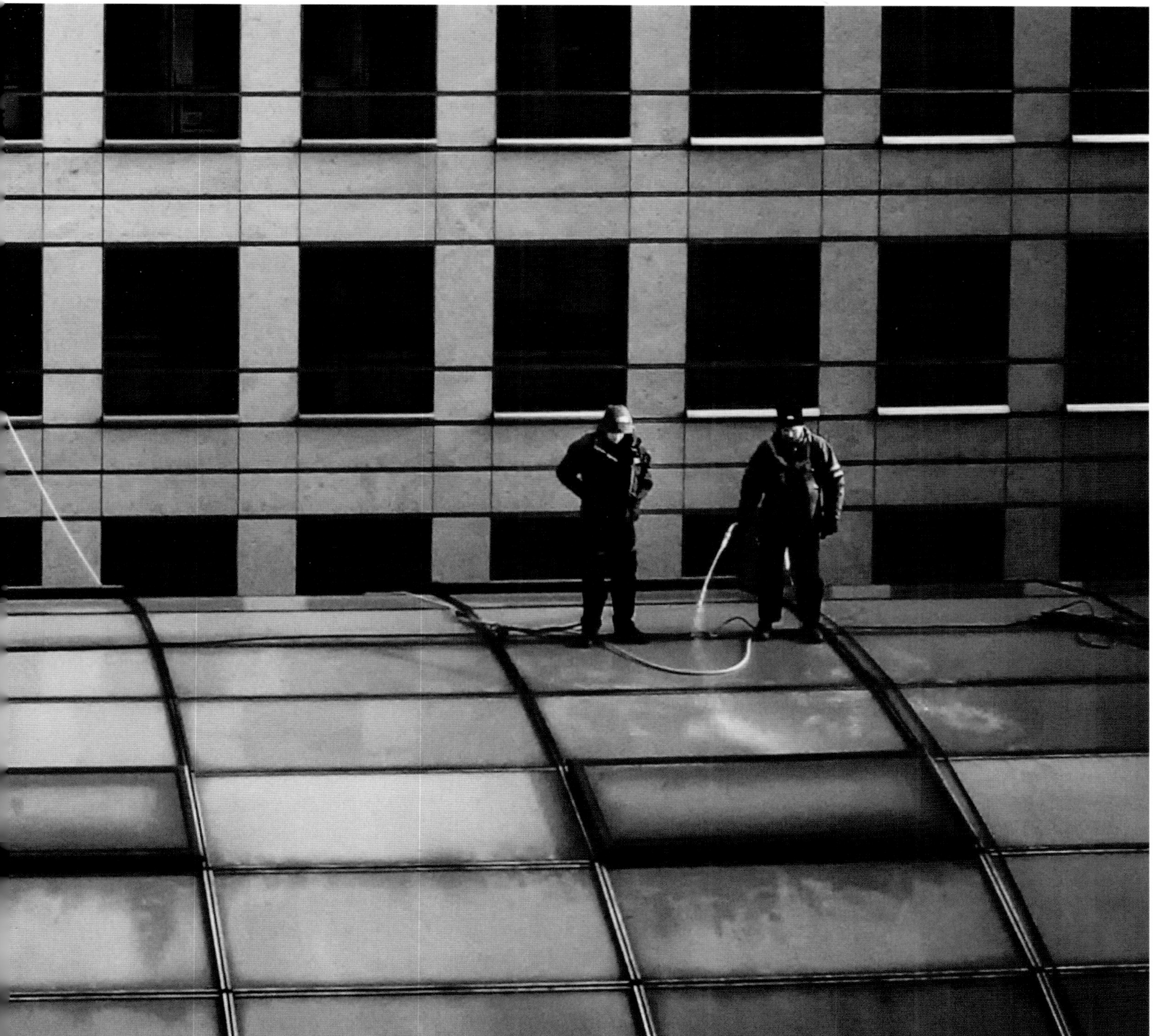

Name: Chris Steel, 45
Nationality: British
Status: Amateur
Photographer since: 2009
Favourite Camera of all Time:
Nikon D3000
Influences: Life

The Location: Cheshire, UK

The Story: It was December 2009, I was on my way to a local supermarket around 10:00 to buy cream cakes as it was my birthday when I saw this maintenance crew repairing some pipework. I returned at lunchtime and asked if it was ok to take some shots while they were working, they said it was. It was bitterly cold, my eyes were streaming and my fingers numb and could barely operate the camera and the guys thought I was nuts. I achieved what I wanted to!

The Exposure:
Camera: Fuji S7000
Lens: F7.8 Fixed
Settings: F2.9 1/60 ISO 200 Focal Length 11mm
Post-production: Paint.net

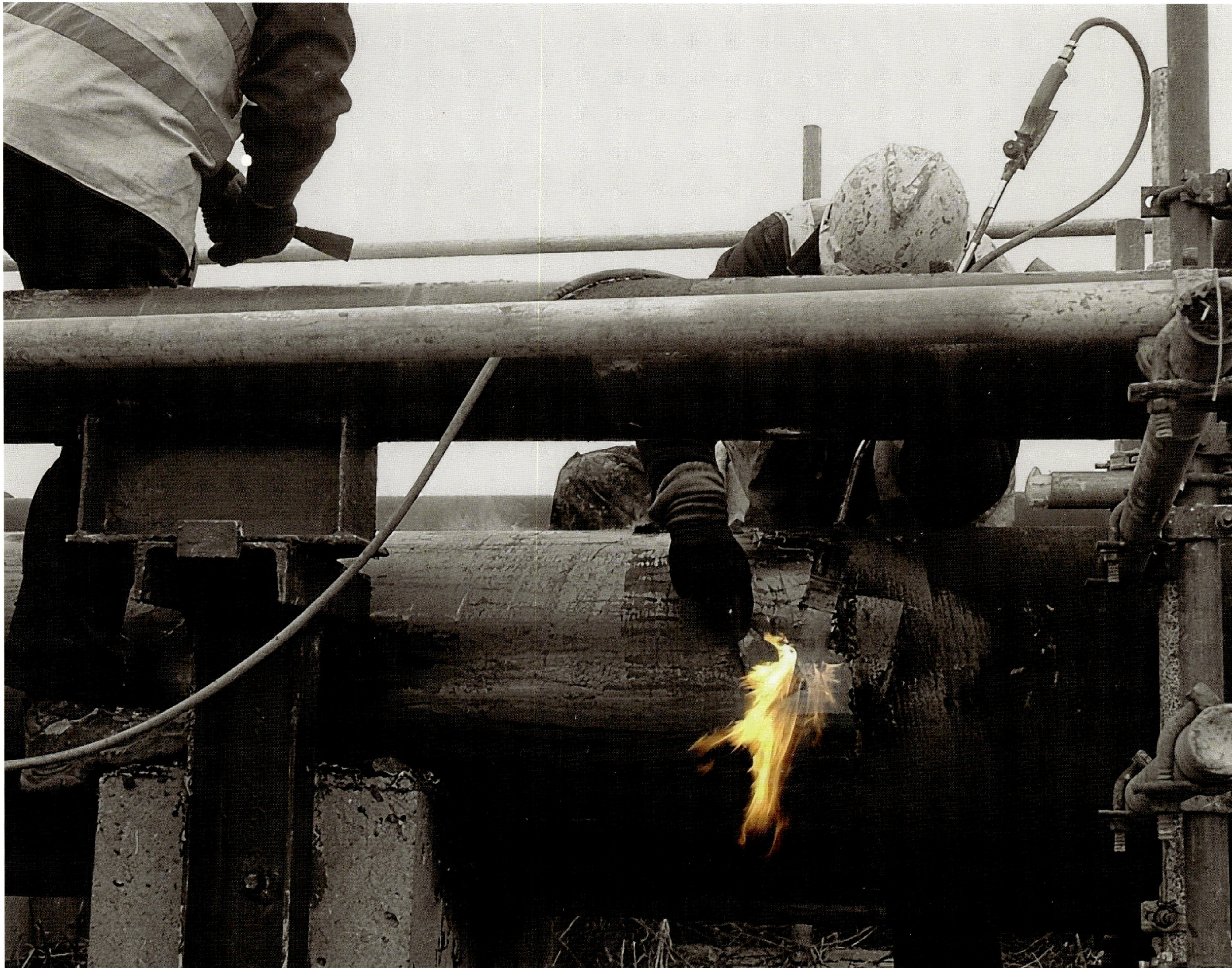

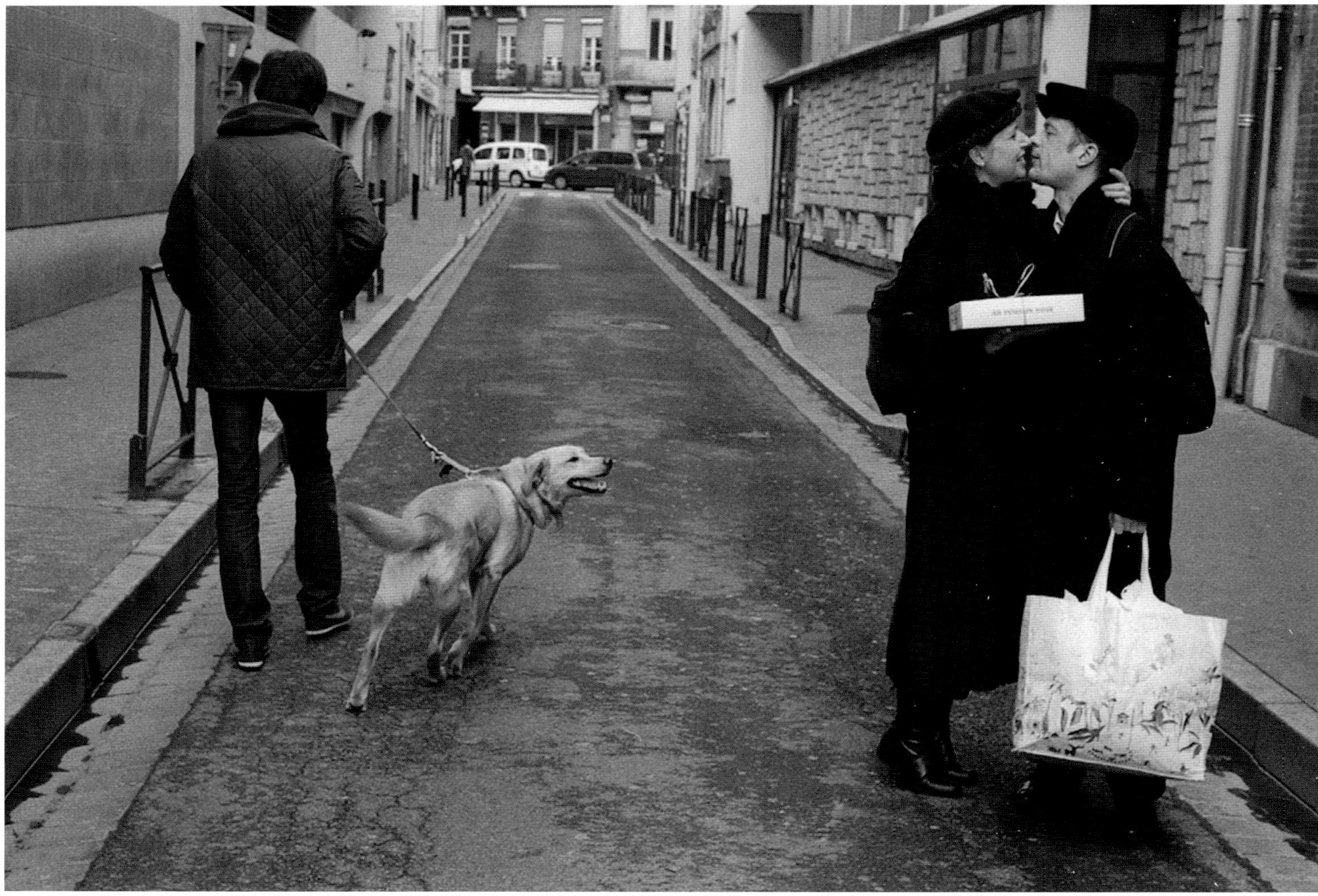

Name: Nathanaël Fournier, 29
Nationality: French
Photographer since: 2003
Favourite Camera of all Time: Leica M6
Influences: Abbas, Boubat, Cartier-Bresson, Riboud, Saul Leiter

The Location: Toulouse, France

The Story: I stopped to capture the couple kissing. I could tell by their body language as they approached each other that that was probably what they would do. The man with the dog wandered into frame as I composed the shot. I did not brief the dog but it is what I would have told him to do if I could have done!

The Exposure:
Camera : Leica M6
Lens: 50mm
Post-production: EpsonScan, Photoshop

Name: Nick Board, 55
Nationality: English
Status: Amateur
Photographer since: 1970
Favourite Camera of all Time: Canon 5D
Influences: Tim Page, Cartier Bresson, Dorothea Lange

The Location: London, UK

The Story: I was visiting Wren's St James's Church in Piccadilly which just happens to have an interesting market going in. I noticed The Maltese High Commisssion reflected in the old Crown glass panels, producing images which I believe are peculiar to this sort of glass. As I happened to have my 5D with me I took a few shots, and I felt this one captured the phenomomen the best.

The Exposure:
Camera: Camera 5D
Lens: 70-300 DO IS at 285mm
Settings: ISO 100 F5.6 1/50 Aperture Priority
Post-production: Photoshop, Lightroom

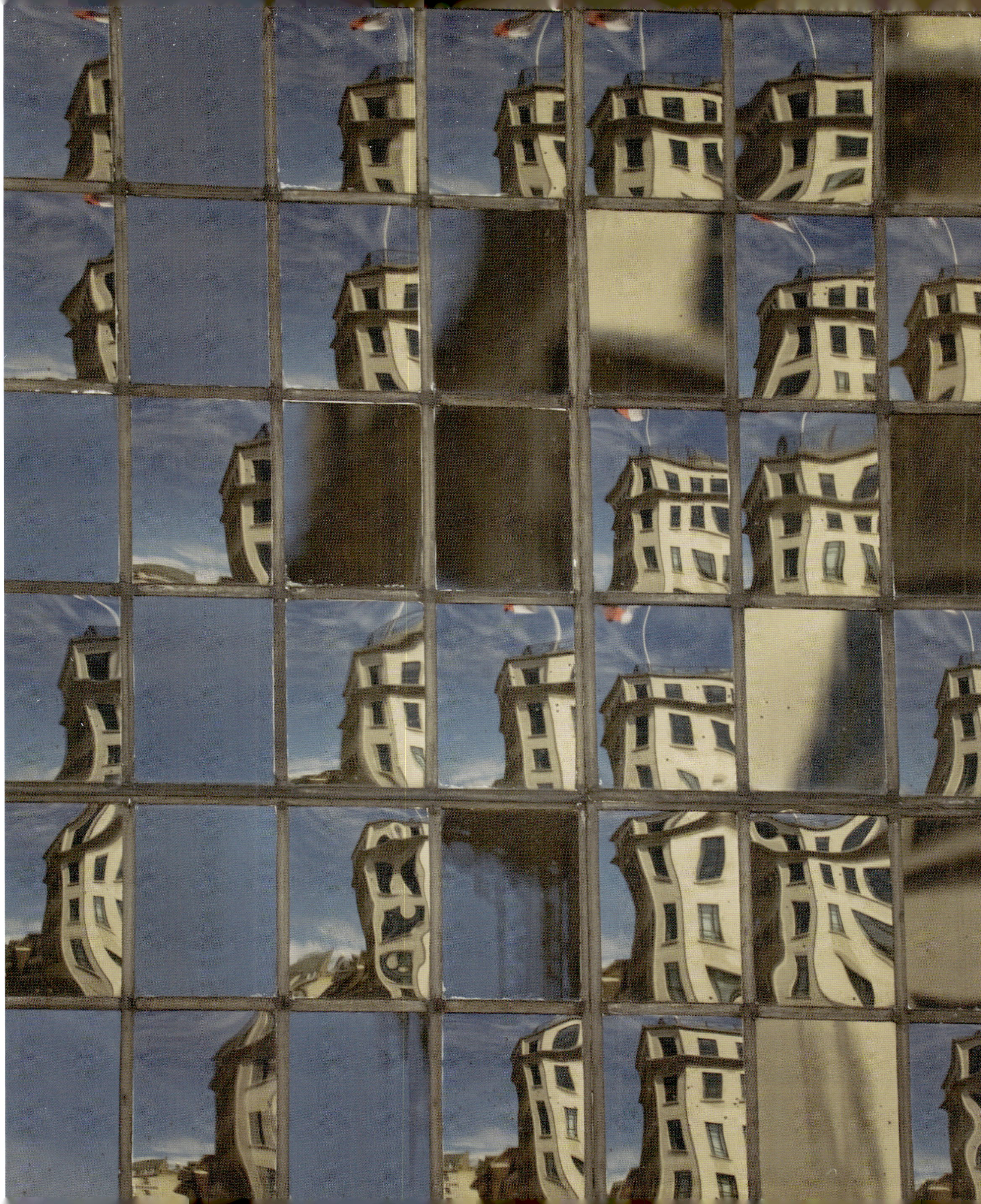

Name: James Lister Sinfield, 33
Nationality: English
Status: Professional
Photographer since: 1996
Favourite Camera of all Time: Olympus OM2
Influences: Richard Feynmann, Paul Dirac, Alfred Hitchcock

The Location: Shropshire, UK

The Story: Whilst strolling around Ludlow looking for some lunch, I walked past a barbers and had to stop and take pictures. For me, this photo is all about the eyebrows. The old boy receiving the haircut was full of bluster and gusto. Almost certainly a retired major.

The Exposure:
Camera: Nikon D70
Lens: Nikkor 50mm 1.4
Settings: F1.8 @ 1/200 sec
Post-production: Photoshop

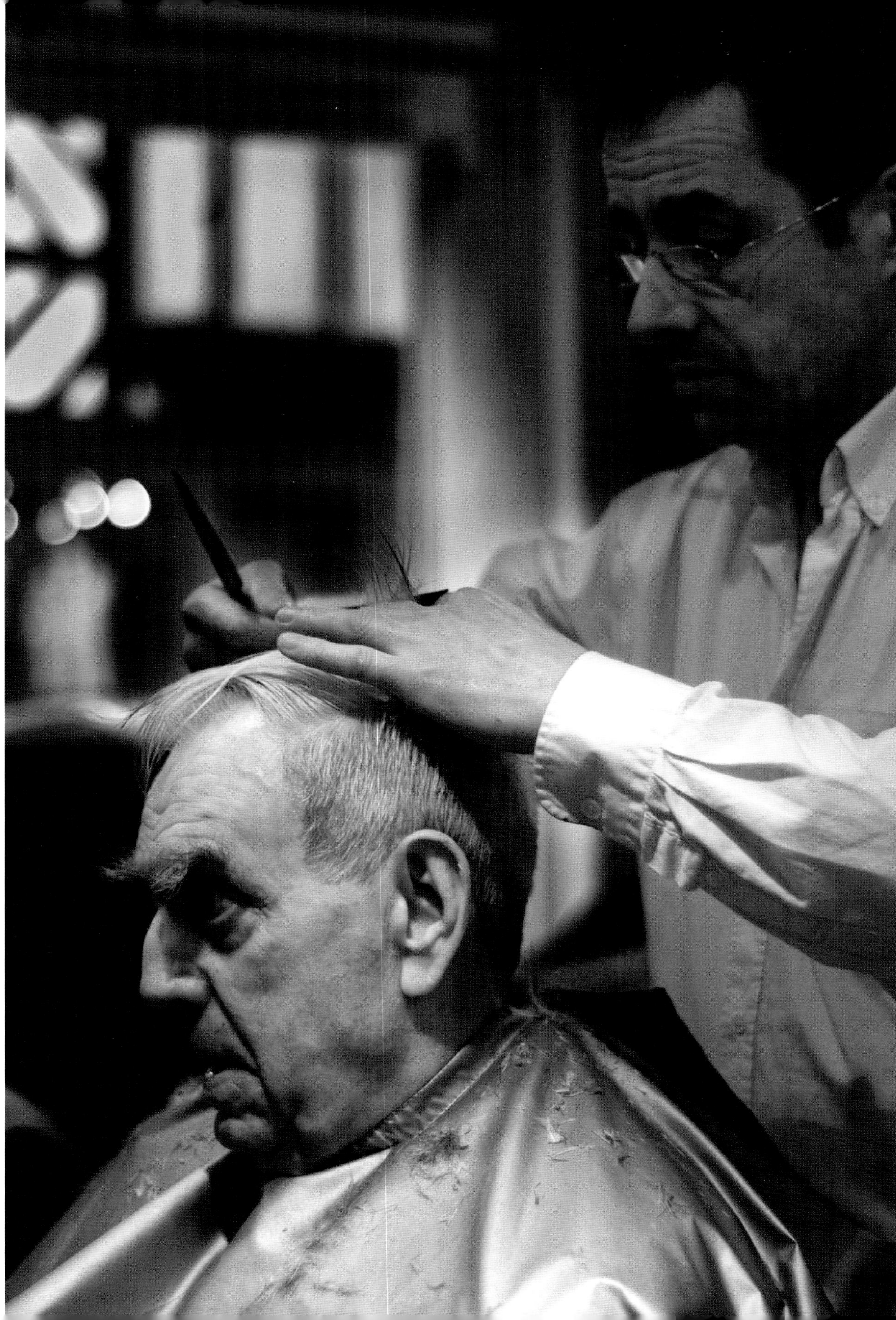

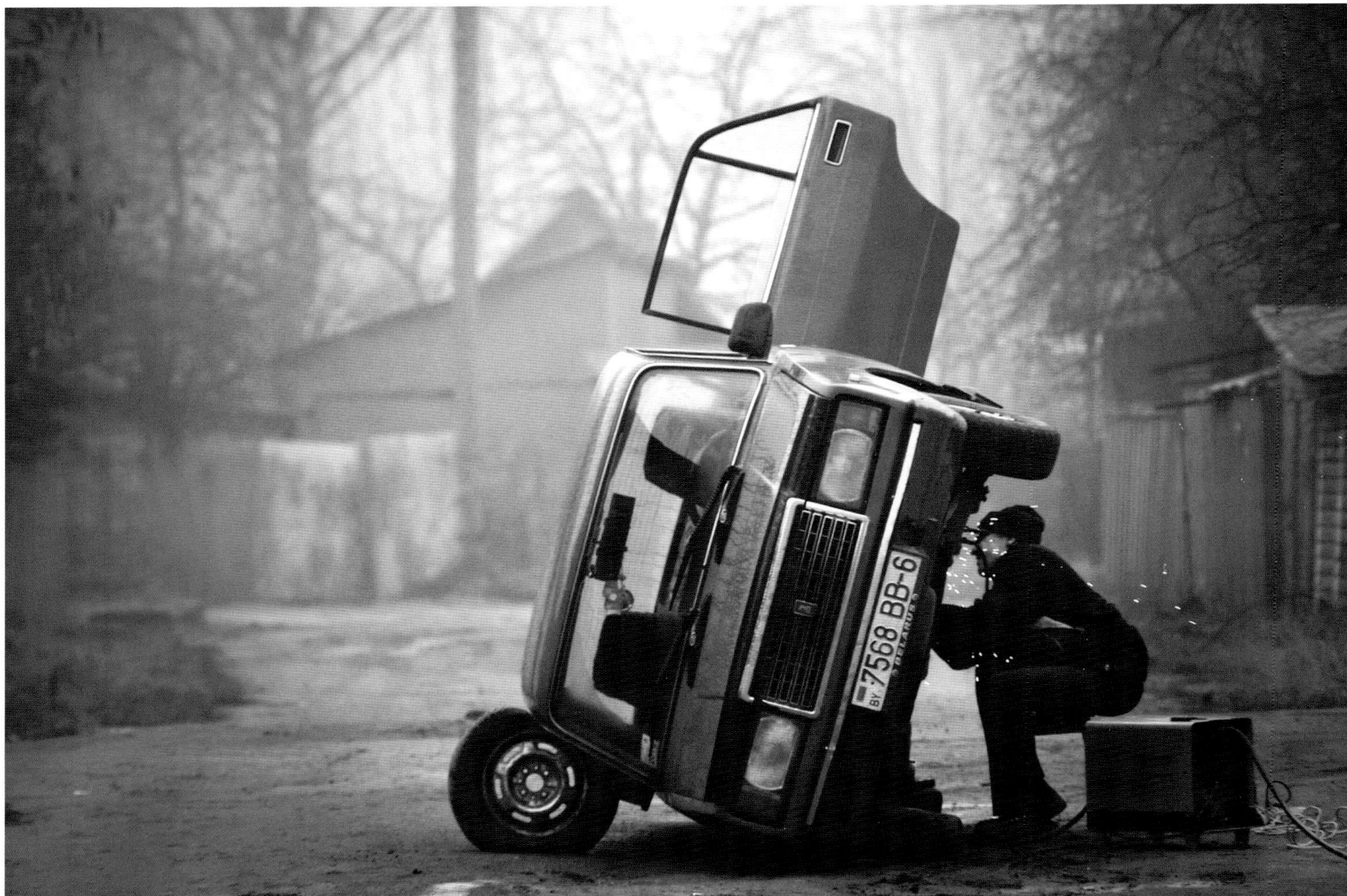
BY
7568 BB-6

Name: Mihail Kopychko, 22
Nationality: Russian
Status: Amateur
Photographer since: 2010
Favourite Camera of all Time: Nikon D90
Influences: Nature

The Location: Belarus, Russia

The Story: This photo I took on the outskirts of the city of Mogilev. A man repairing an old Russian Lada car in front of his house in an unusual way. Such repairs can often be seen in our area. When I brought a printed photograph to this man, he was very pleased and the car was in excellent condition!

The Exposure:
Camera: Nikon D60
Lens: Yupiter 21m 200mm F/4
Settings: F4 @ 1/200 sec ISO 200
Post-production: Photoshop

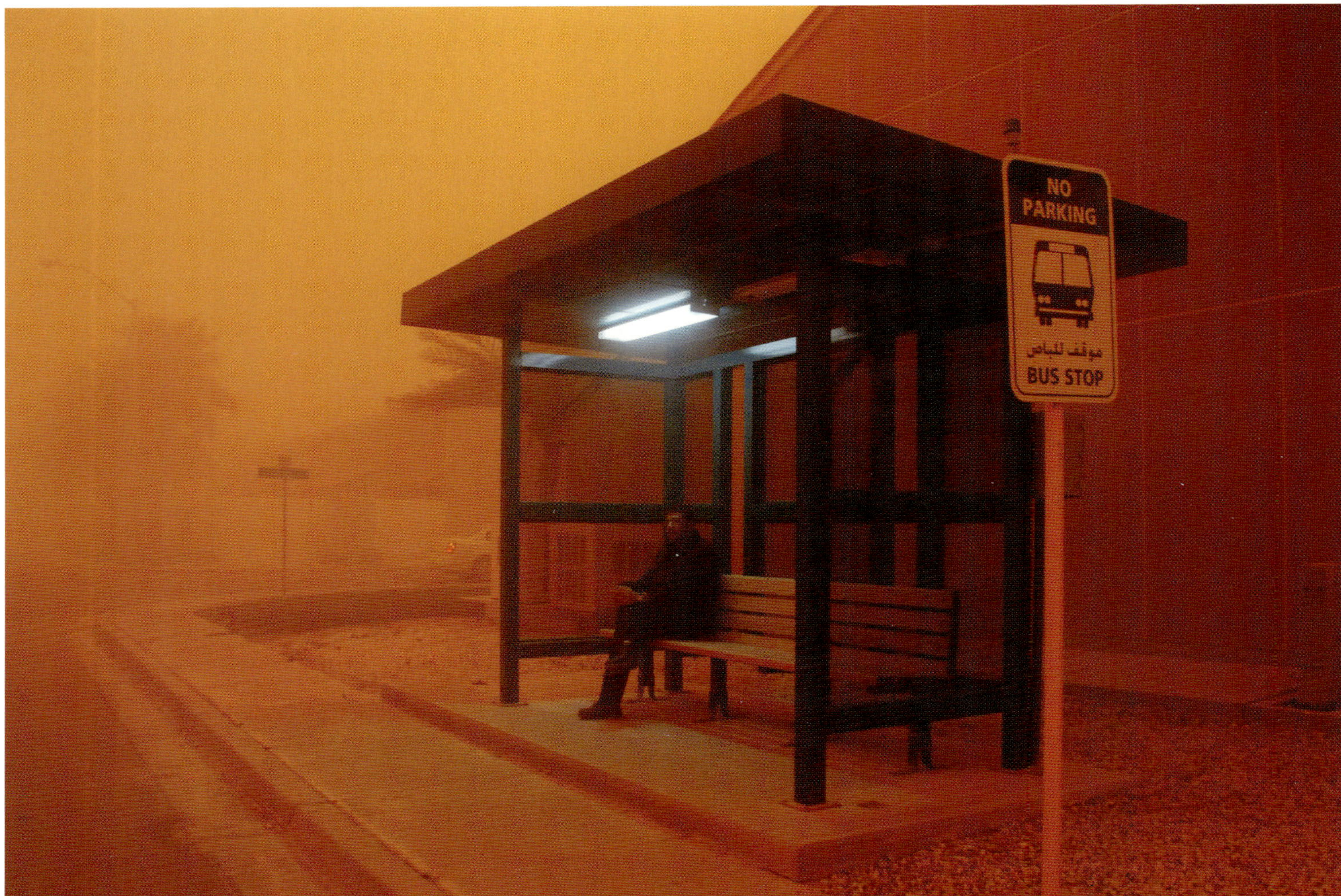
NO PARKING
موقف للباص
BUS STOP

Name: Hussain A. Al-jassim, 26
Nationality: Saudi Arabian
Status: Amateur
Photographer since: 2008
Favourite Camera of all Time: Nikon D80
Influences: Larry Burrows, David Hobby

The Location: Saudi Arabia

The Story: During a particularly bad storm, there was a person waiting for the bus to go to work. This picture highlights the person's dedication to their job.

The Exposure:
Camera: Nikon D80
Post-production: Photoshop, Nik Sharpener

Name: Lukas Macek, 25
Nationality: Slovakian
Status: Professional
Photographer since: 2005
Favourite Camera of all Time: Pentacon Six
Influences: H.Cartier-Bresson

The Location: Southend-on-Sea, UK

The Story: I took this candid shot while passing through the main street and looking for some interesting reflections in shop windows. Luckily for me, the lady was just redecorating it.

The Exposure:
Camera: Canon 350D
Lens: 18-55, F3.5-5.6
Settings: F7.1 @ 1/80 sec ISO 200
Post-production: Photoshop

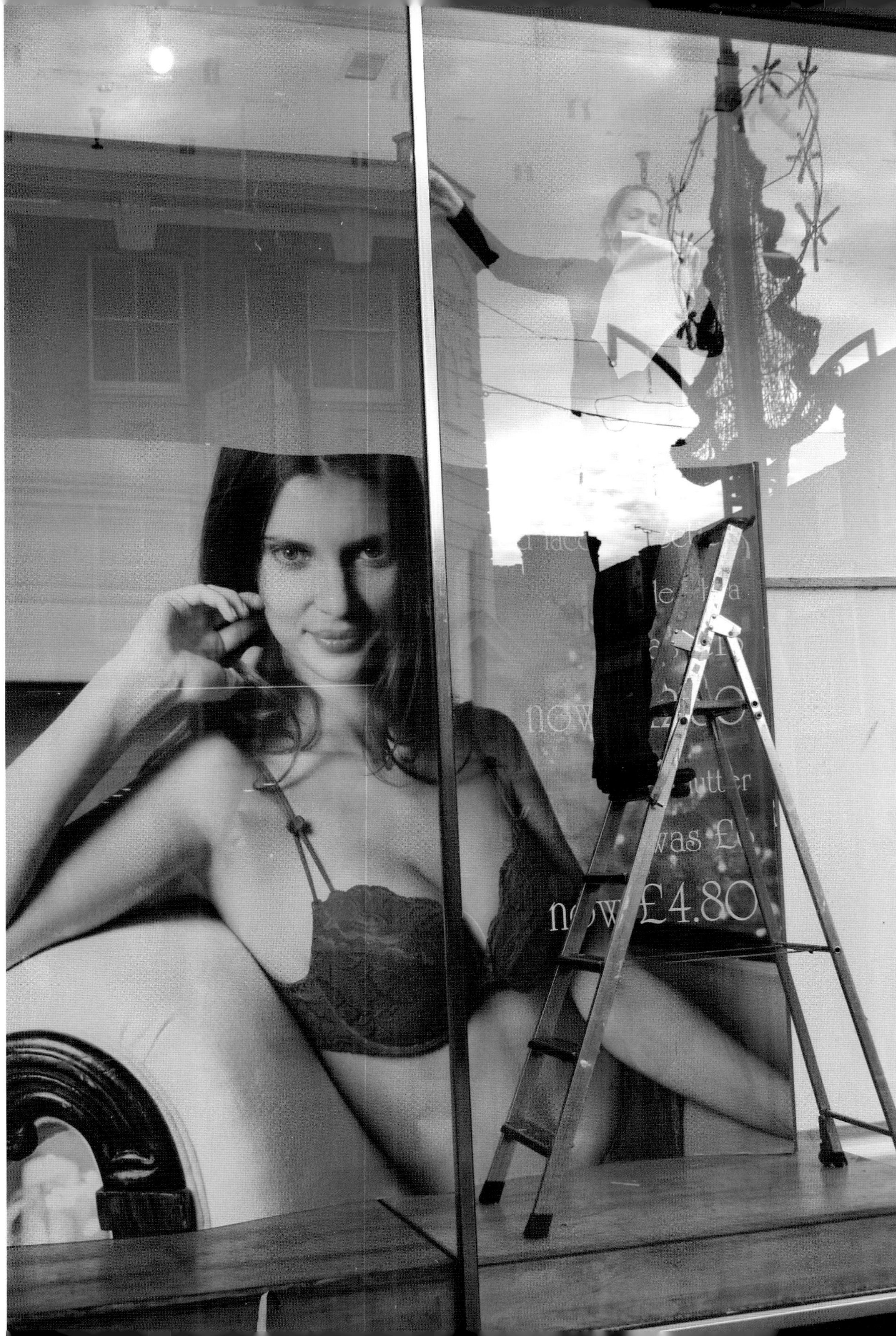

22 23

Name: Jose Luis Morales Martin, 39
Nationality: Spanish
Status: Amateur
Photographer since: 2007
Favourite Camera of all Time:
Canon EOS 5D Mark II
Influences: Josep Hoflehner,
David Zimmermna, Peter Lik

The Location: Cantabria, Spain

The Story: We were spending the summer holidays in Cantabria and suddenly a sheep flock appeared in the main street with a long queue of cars behind them. All the people were amazed. Nowadays, in Spain, there are many old paths for cattle and sheep and you do not see many crossing the cities!

The Exposure:
Camera: Nikon D80
Lens: Tamron 18-250 at 50mm
Settings: F/9 1/125s. ISO 200
Post-production: Nikon capture NX

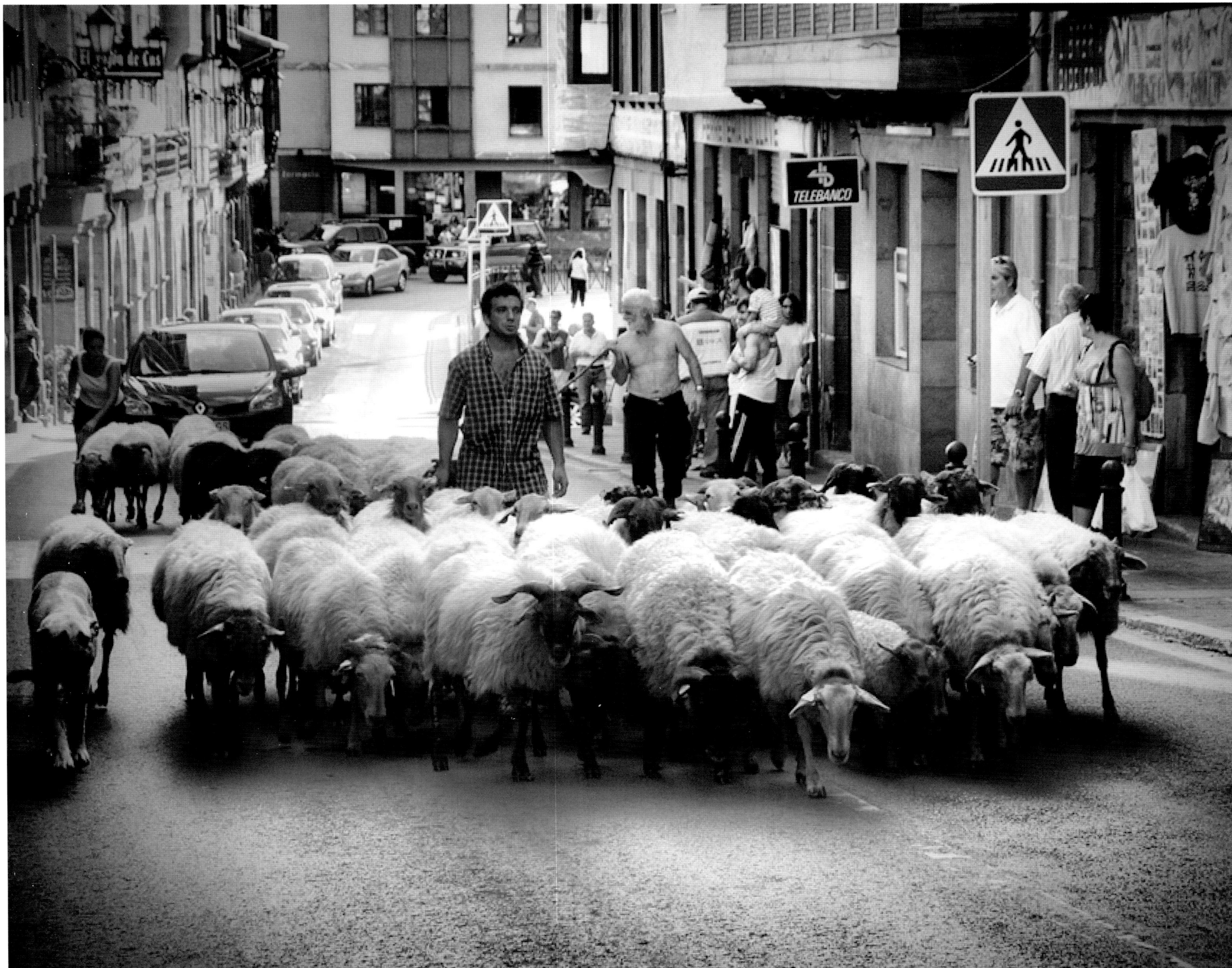
TELEBANCO

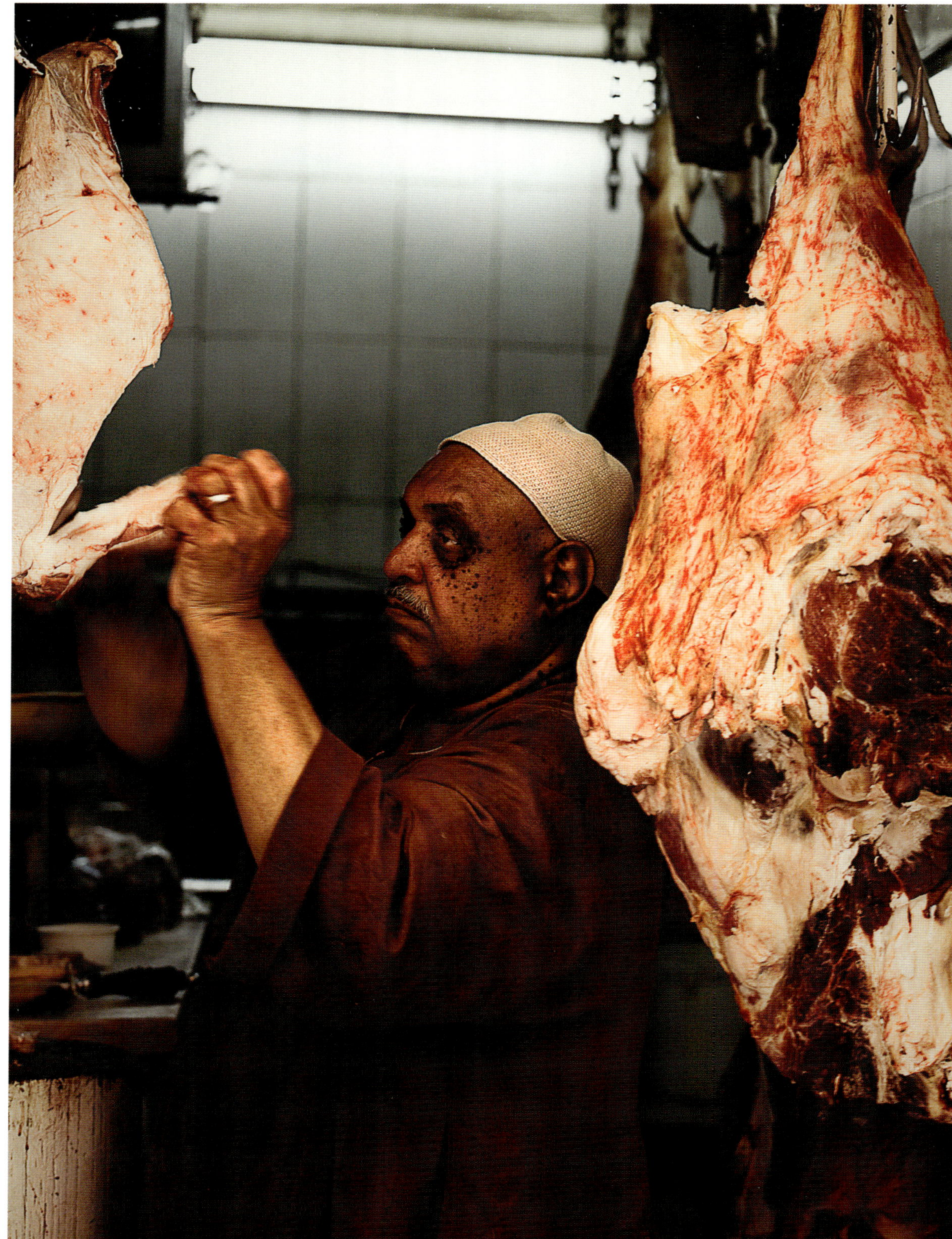

Name: Nigel Eberhardt, 26
Nationality: Australian
Status: Amateur
Photographer since: 2007
Favourite Camera of all Time: 20x24 Polaroid
Influences: Ansel Adams, Phil Gallagher, Chris Burkard

The Location: Luxor, Egypt

The Story: This image was taken in a busy bazaar in Luxor, Egypt. I set myself a brief this particular day, which was to attempt to capture the day to day life in the bazaar as accurately as I could. This particular man was a perfect subject. His face expressionless as he laboured on butchering meat. The image he provided struck me as having such a contrast to the world I know. I decided to have a coffee at the cafe across the road and watch him going about his work, in the late afternoon. I waited for the perfect moment to capture the scene and draw attention to the motions of his hands by using an extended shutter speed.

The Exposure:
Camera: Canon 5D Mark 2
Lens: 70-200mm F4.0/L
Settings: F5 @ 1/60 sec ISO 400
Post-production: Photoshop, Lightroom

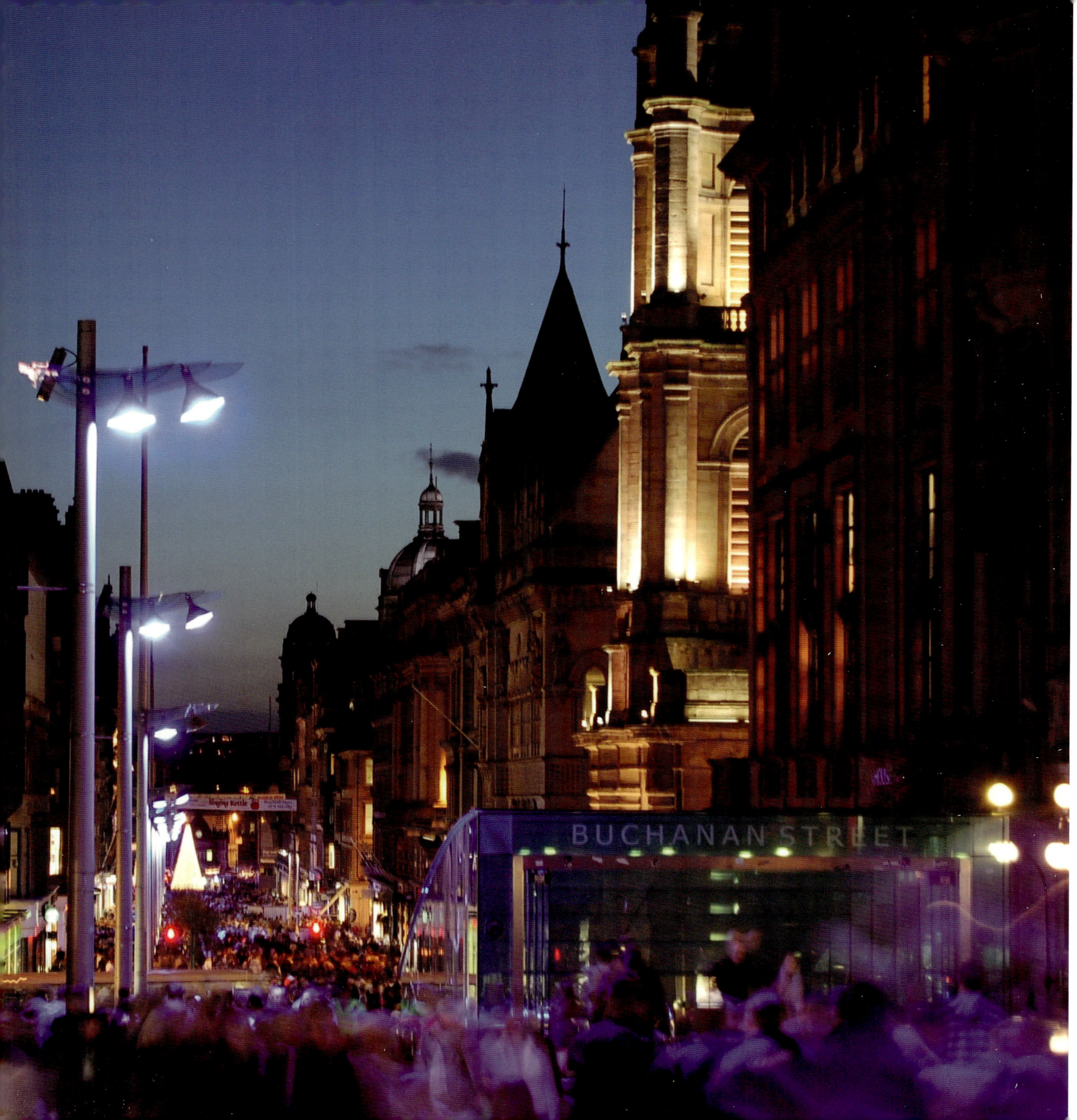
BUCHANAN STREET

Name: David O'Hare, 25
Nationality: Scottish
Status: Amateur
Photographer since: 2005
Favourite Camera of all Time: Nikon D90
Influences: Harry Benson, Russell Davies

The Location: Glasgow, UK

The Story: As Glasgow's busiest and most iconic street, Buchanan Street is just full of life. I didn't have a tripod with me, so I placed my camera on top of a pretty grubby bin, pointed it towards the subway station, and hoped for the best. Despite the strange looks I got, it was worth it.

The Exposure:
Camera: Nikon D50
Lens: F5.6 @ 1.3 sec ISO 200
Post-production: Microsoft Picture It 10

Name: Nathanaël Fournier, 29
Nationality: French
Status: Amateur
Photographer since: 2003
Favourite Camera of all Time: Leica M6
Influences: Abbas, Boubat, Cartier-Bresson, Riboud, Saul Leiter

The Location: Paris, France

The Story: It is true that I was on autopilot when I took this photo. I was hurrying between assignments and crossed the road ahead of their bike, making them stop. It was not until I got home that I saw the 'little girl excitement' on the woman's face and wondered why she was having such fun - the mind makes up beautiful stories.

The Exposure:
Camera: Leica M6
Lens: 50mm
Post-production: EpsonScan, Photoshop

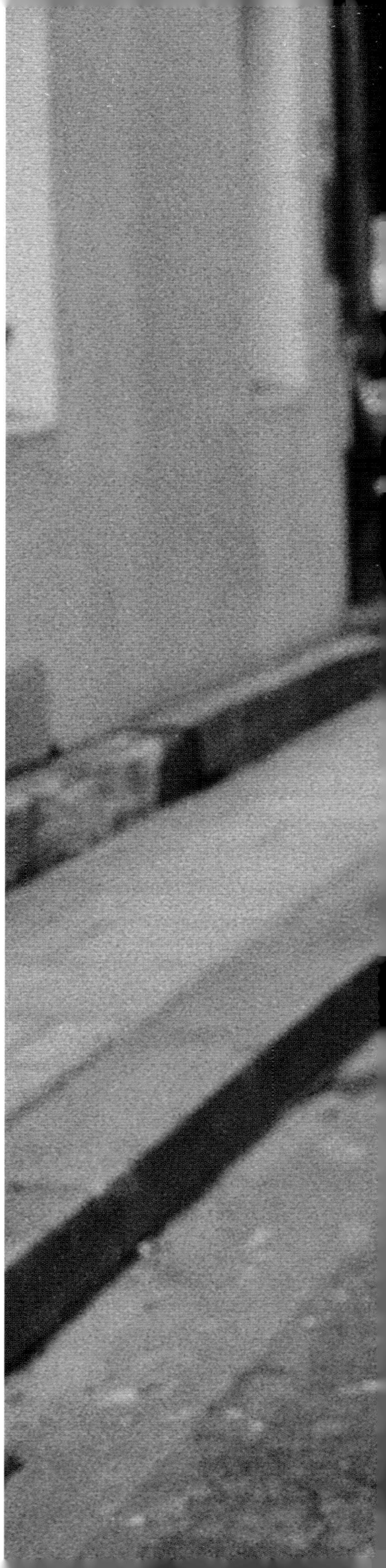

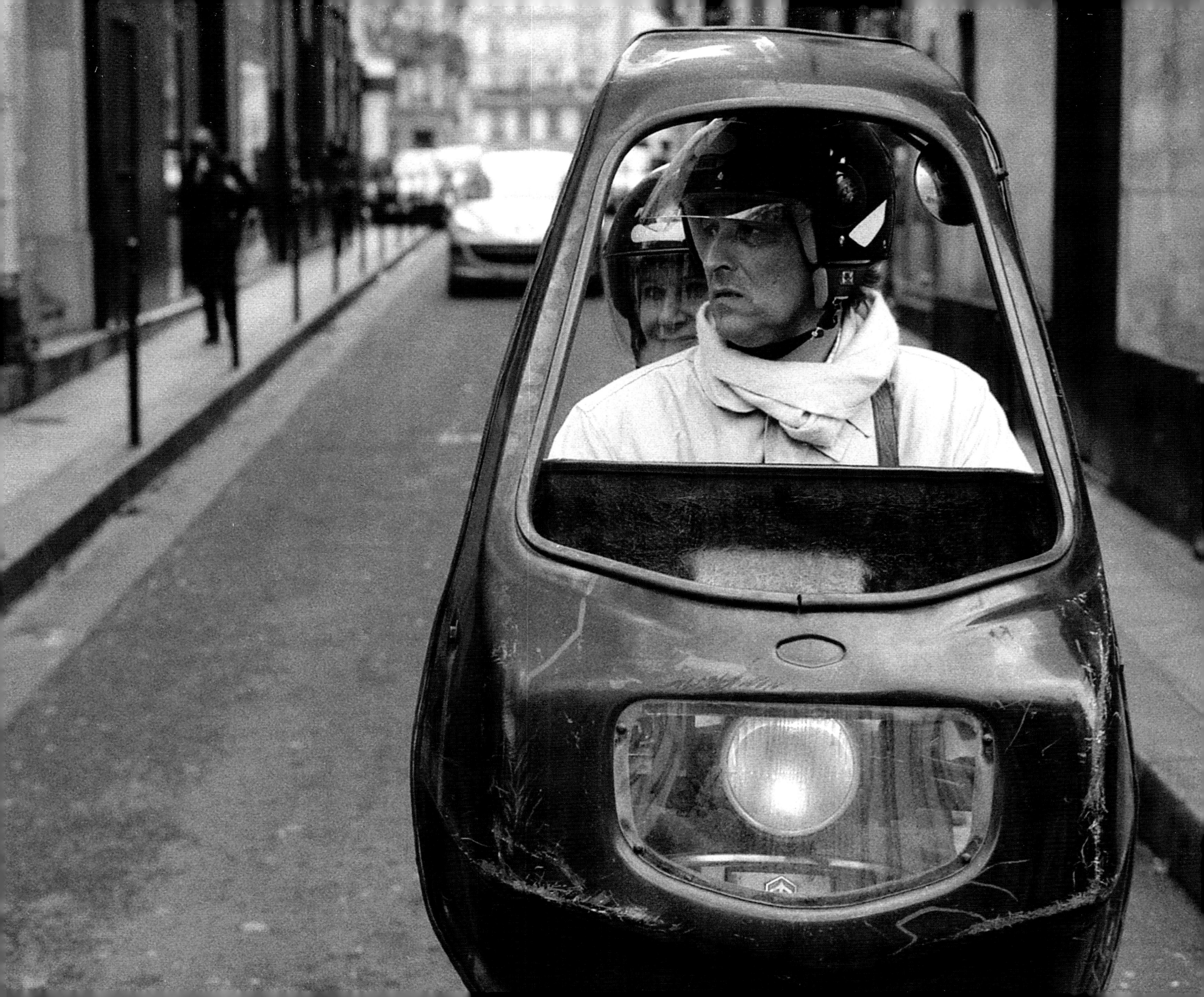

Name: Mohammad Esmaeeli, 28
Nationality: Iranian
Status: Amateur
Photographer since: 2006
Favourite Camera of all Time:
Canon 5D Mark II
Influences: Richard Avedon

The Location: Tehran, Iran

The Story: I live in Tehran, a city in which it doesn't snow much. When I woke up on a cold winter day and saw the city covered with snow, I decided to take my camera. On my way back home from work, I stumbled across a parking lot where the police keep impounded cars and bikes.

The Exposure:
Camera: Nikon D50
Lens: Nikkor 18-55mm F3/5-5/6
Settings: F8 @ 1/125 sec ISO 200
Post-production: Photoshop

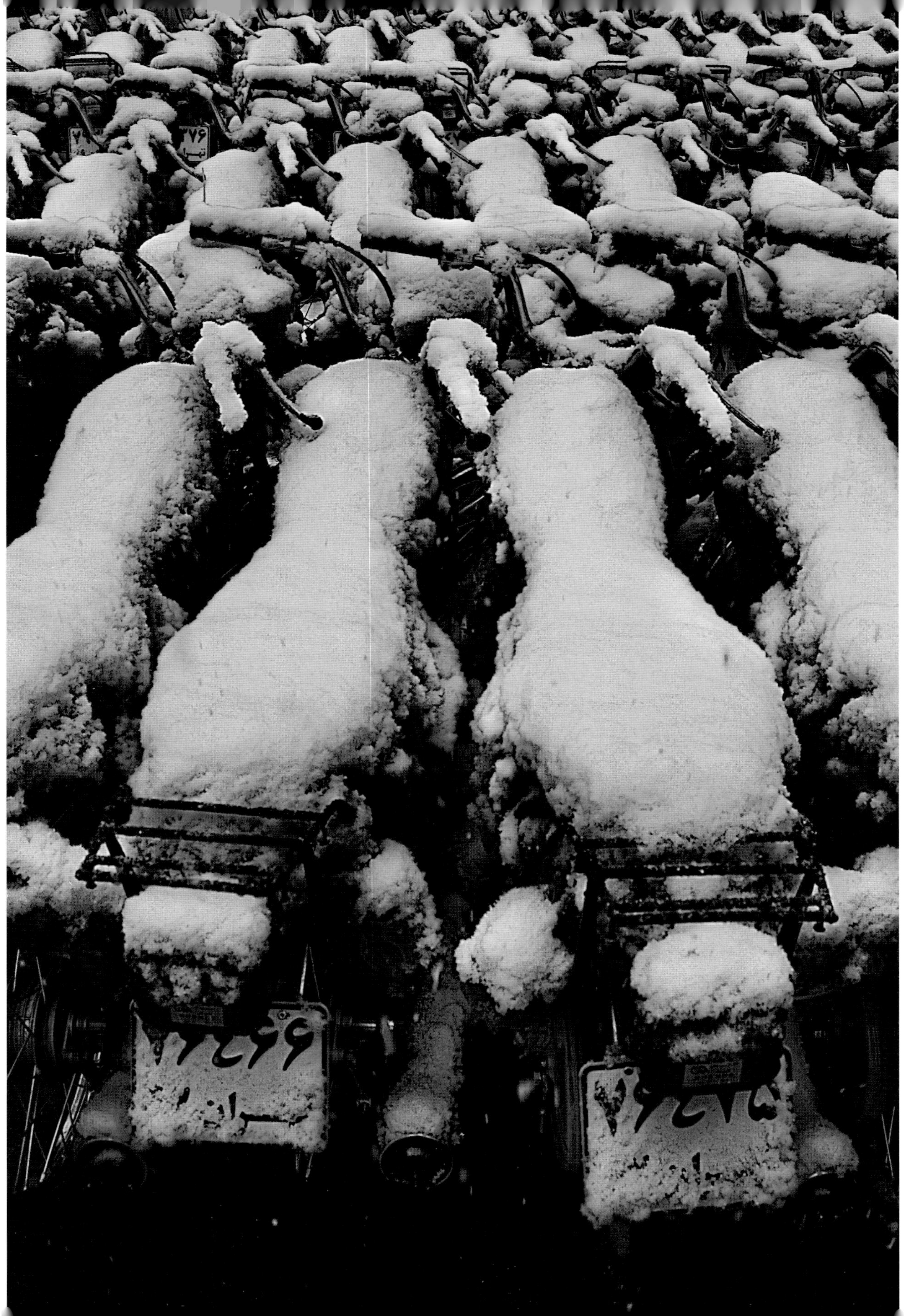

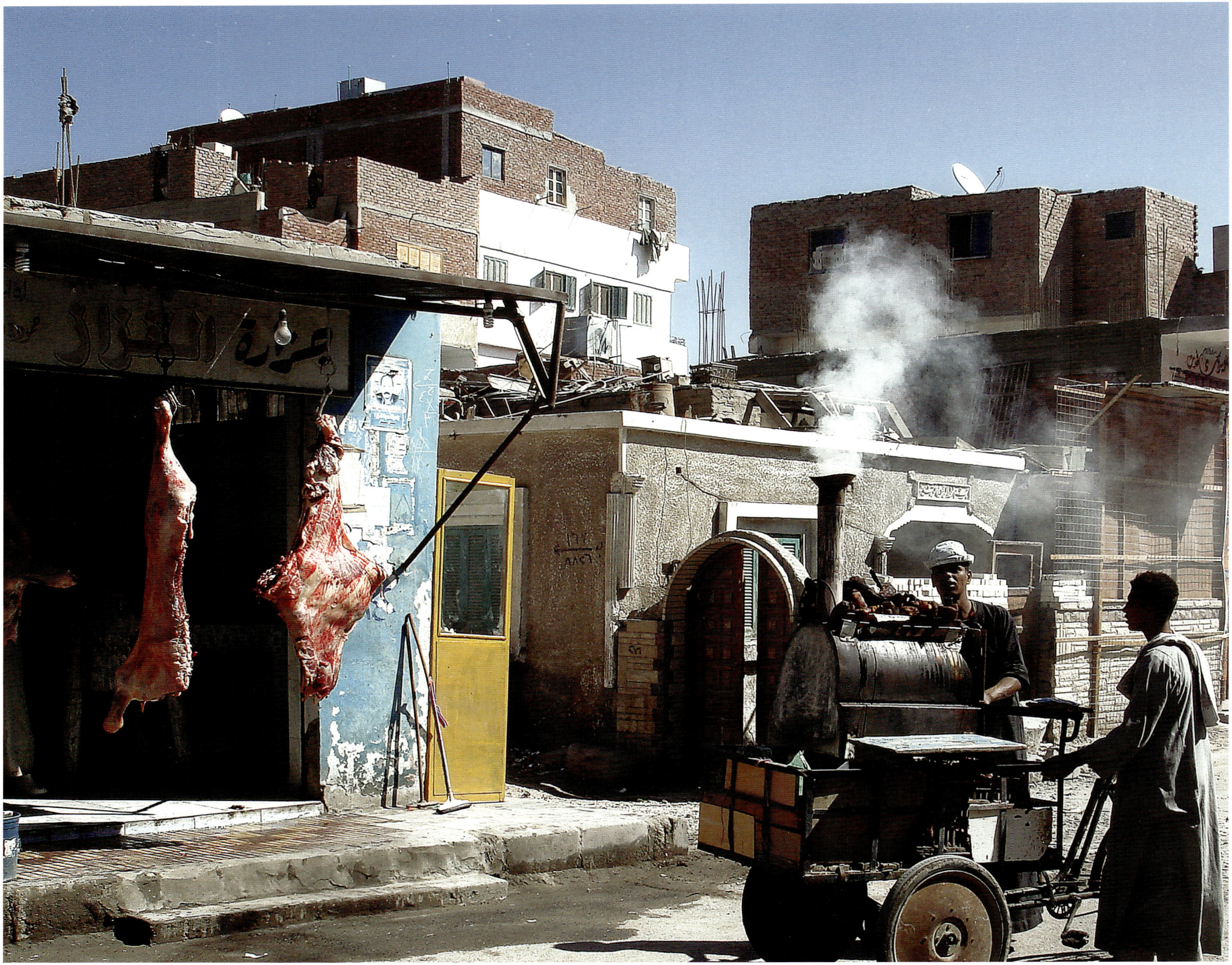

Name: Vincent Peal, 45
Nationality: Belgian
Status: Amateur
Photographer since: 2006
Favourite Camera of all Time: Canon S90
Influences: Weegee, Enrique Metinides

The Location: Hurghada, Egypt

The Story: I was walking in the old city of Hurghada and noticed the carcasses hanging from the hooks. The contrast of the meat against the colour of the building really caught my eye.

The Exposure:
Camera: Canon S90
Lens: 3.8x15
Settings: Auto ISO 800
Post-production: Photoshop

Name: Ana Braganca, 27
Nationality: Portuguese
Status: Amateur
Photographer since: 1998
Favourite Camera of all Time: Nikon D5100
Influences: Steven Meisel, Bansky, Francis Bacon

The Location: Baixa do Porto, Portugal

The Story: This picture was taken in Porto, during an event that's called "Se esta rua fosse minha..." ("If this street was mine..."). The purpose is to promote all kind of artistic events in an ordinary small street. 400 metres along we saw theatre, listened to music, played traditional games, photographed, danced, painted, sang, shopped, etc. The ordinary street was ours for one day. The lady in the photo, who clearly lives nearby, she was simply observing how different that familiar place was.

The Exposure:
Camera: Panasonic DMC-ZS5 12 Megapixel Lumix Digital Camera
Post-production: Photoshop

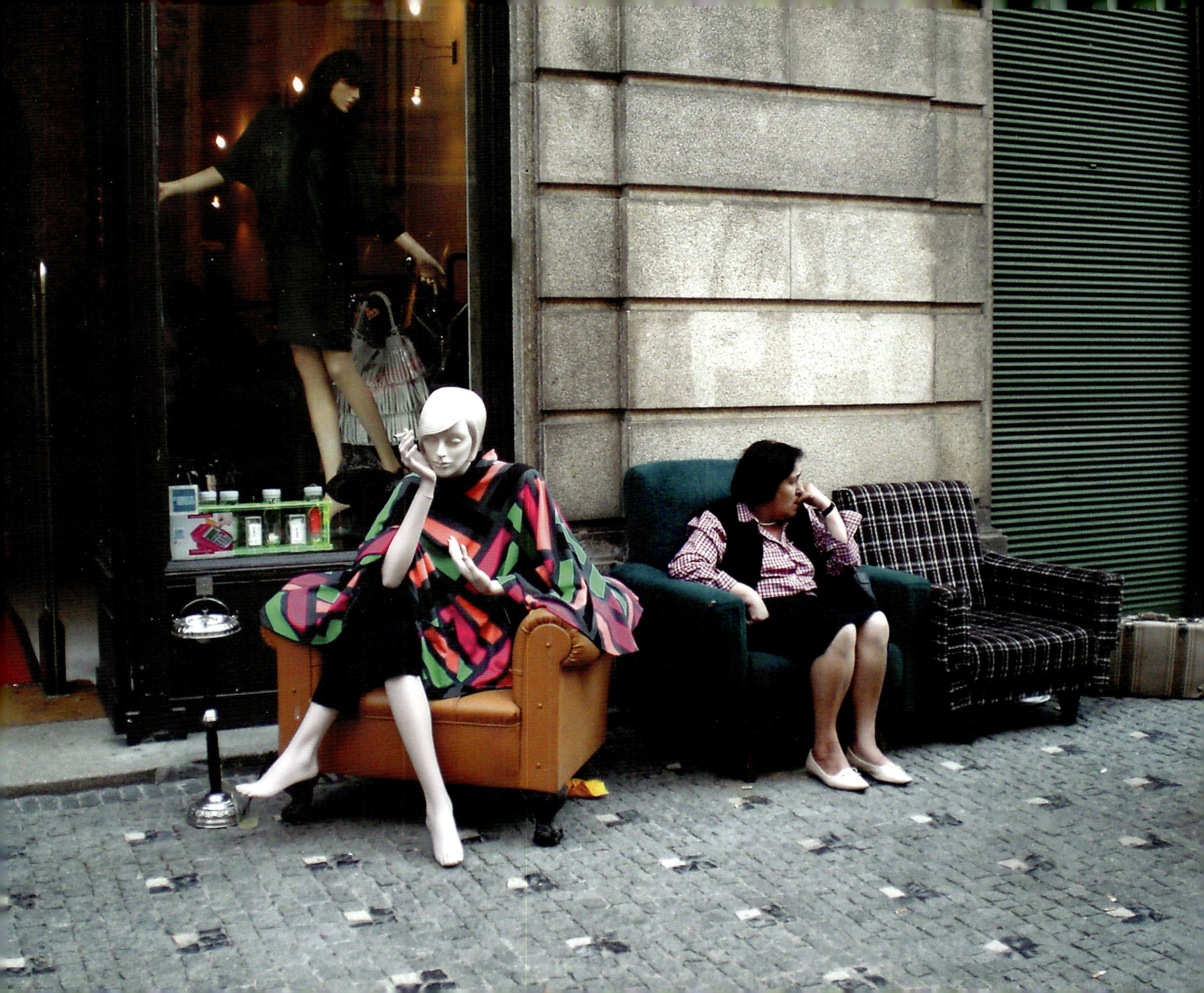

Name: Tony Smith, 48
Nationality: English
Status: Amateur
Photographer since: 1981
Favourite Camera of all Time:
Olympus Om4TI
Influences: David Hockney, Bob Carlos Clark, Bill Brandt

The Location: Cheshire, UK

The Story: I have admired this bridge for many years and photographed it many times in daylight. On this evening I was returning to my car from the centre of the city and saw a number of office workers crossing it to go home. I waited until the dusk light was right and caught the next man crossing.

The Exposure:
Camera: Canon 5DmkII
Lens: Sigma 12-24mm at 12mm
Settings: F11 @ 1/8 sec ISO 400
Post-production: Photoshop

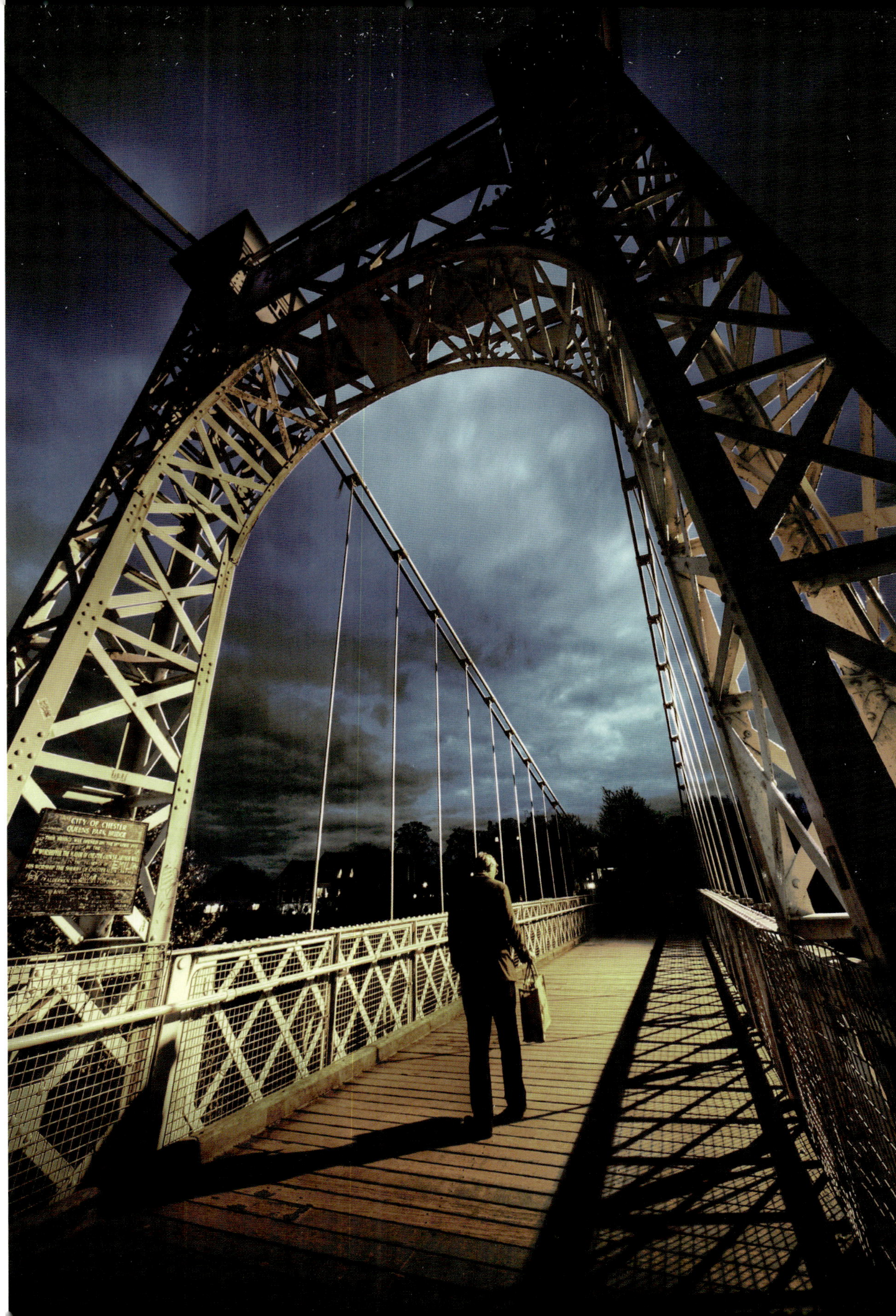
CITY OF CHESTER
QUEENS PARK BRIDGE

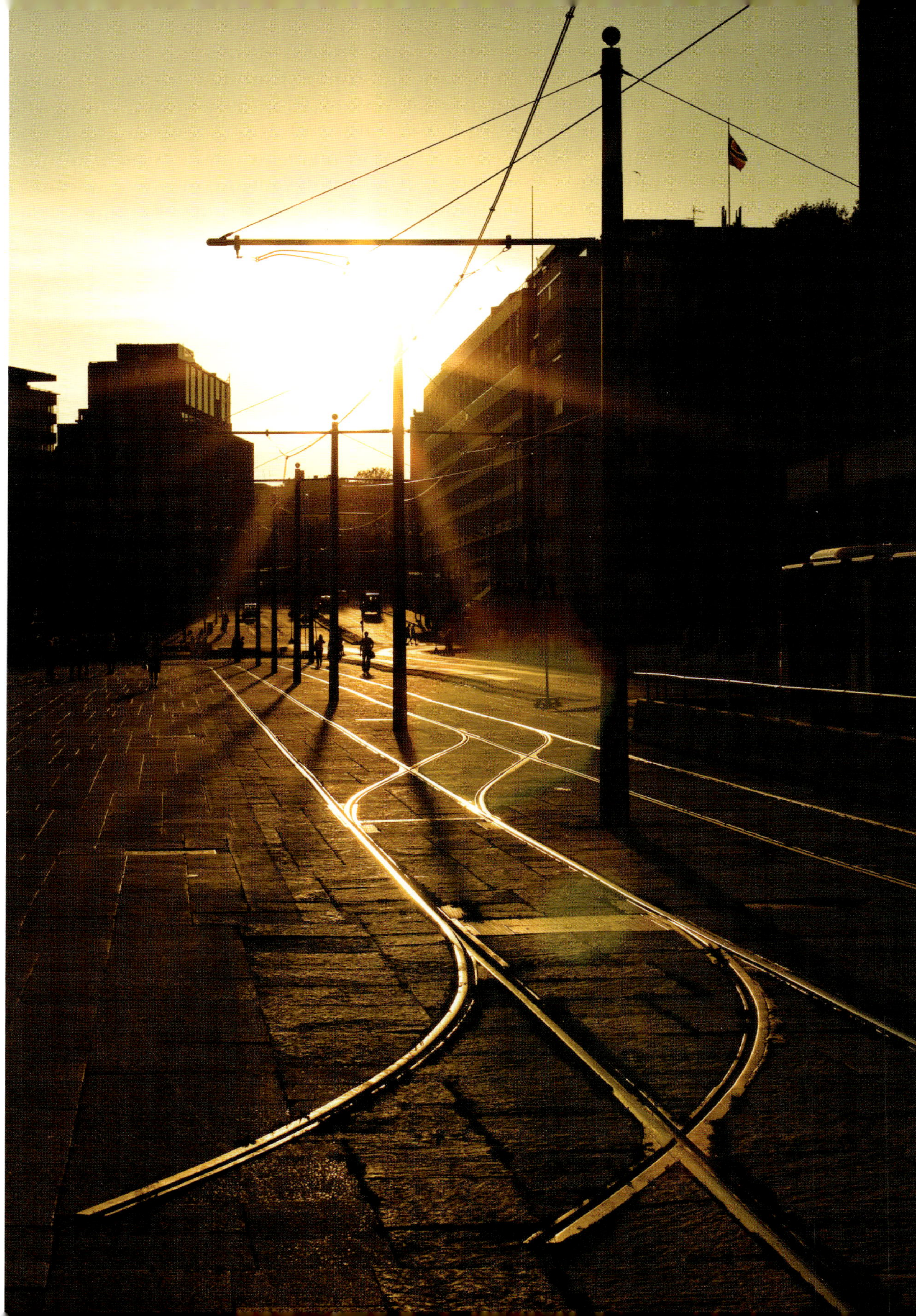

Name: Marianne Lind, 37
Nationality: Norwegian
Status: Professional
Photographer since: 2005
Favourite Camera of all Time: Nikon D700
Influences: Sebastiao Salgado, Elliot Erwitt, Helmut Newton

The Location: Oslo, Norway

The Story: I was just out for a walk downtown one evening, when the light suddenly turned beautiful. The old tram tracks were glowing in the sunset, and leading the eye to the silhouettes of people further into the picture. The picture has more of a feel than a story.

The Exposure:
Camera: Nikon D700
Lens: 50mm F:1.4
Settings: F8 @ 1/320 sec ISO 200
Post-production: Photoshop

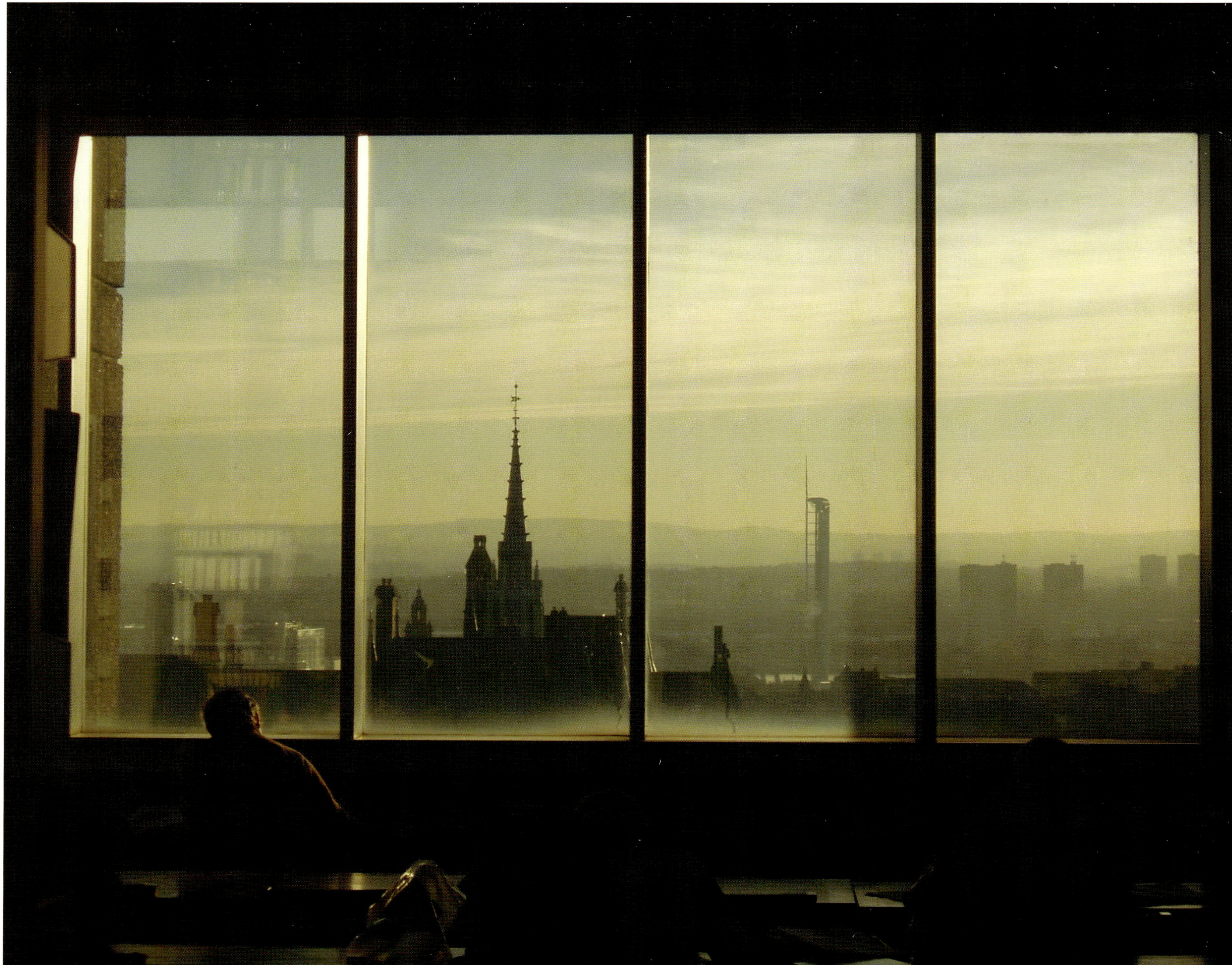

Name: David O'Hare, 25
Nationality: Scottish
Status: Amateur
Photographer since: 2005
Favourite Camera of all Time: Nikon D90
Influences: Harry Benson, Russell Davies

The Location: Glasgow, UK

The Story: The views from Glasgow University's library are stunning, especially around sunset. Having wanted to capture the atmosphere of the 11th floor since the day I first stumbled across it, I finally plucked up the courage to bring my compact camera and take a couple of shots, and got rather lucky with this one.

The Exposure:
Camera: Olympus MJU 400
Lens: F3.1-5.2
Settings: F4.5 @ 1/200 sec ISO 64
Post-production: Microsoft Picture It 10w

Name: Julius Koivistoinen, 20
Nationality: Finnish
Status: Photography Student
Photographer since: 2007
Favourite Camera of all Time:
Hasselblad 503
Influences: Larry Burrows, David Hobby,
Erik Almås

The Location: St. Petersburg, Russia

The Story: The bus and tram windows were often covered in a thick fog which made the whole scene look like it was from a film noir movie. Also the reflections in them gave me the opportunity of seeing things from two perspectives at once. It was very dark out there. The St. Petersburg main street shops were full of customers and there were massive amounts of beautiful light everywhere.

The Exposure:
Camera: Canon EOS 5D
Lens: EF 14-40mm F/4L
Settings: F4 @ 1/200 sec ISO 3200
Post-production: Adobe Lightroom

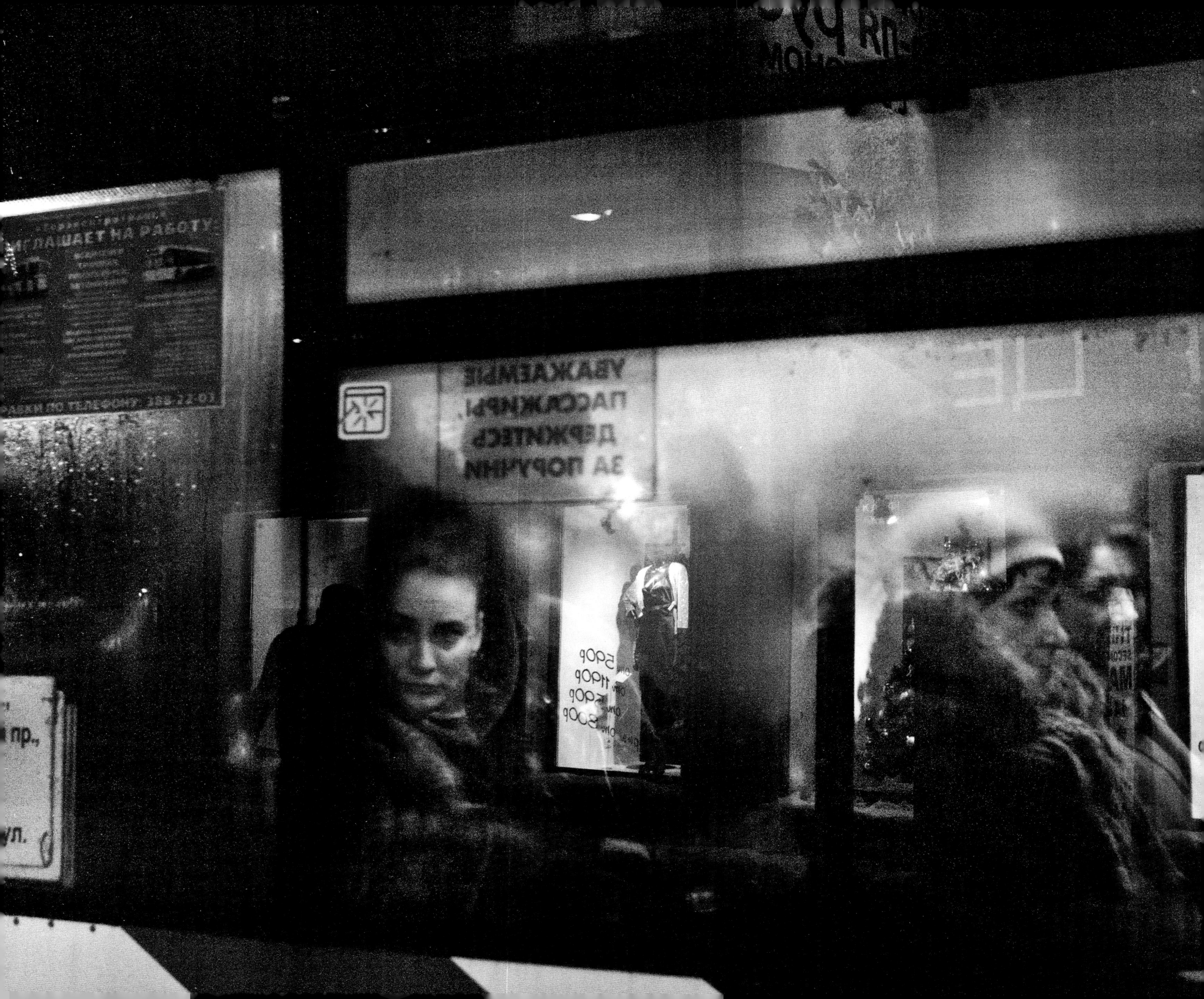
ГЛАШАЕТ НА РАБОТУ
УВАЖАЕМЫЕ ПАССАЖИРЫ, ДЕРЖИТЕСЬ ЗА ПОРУЧНИ

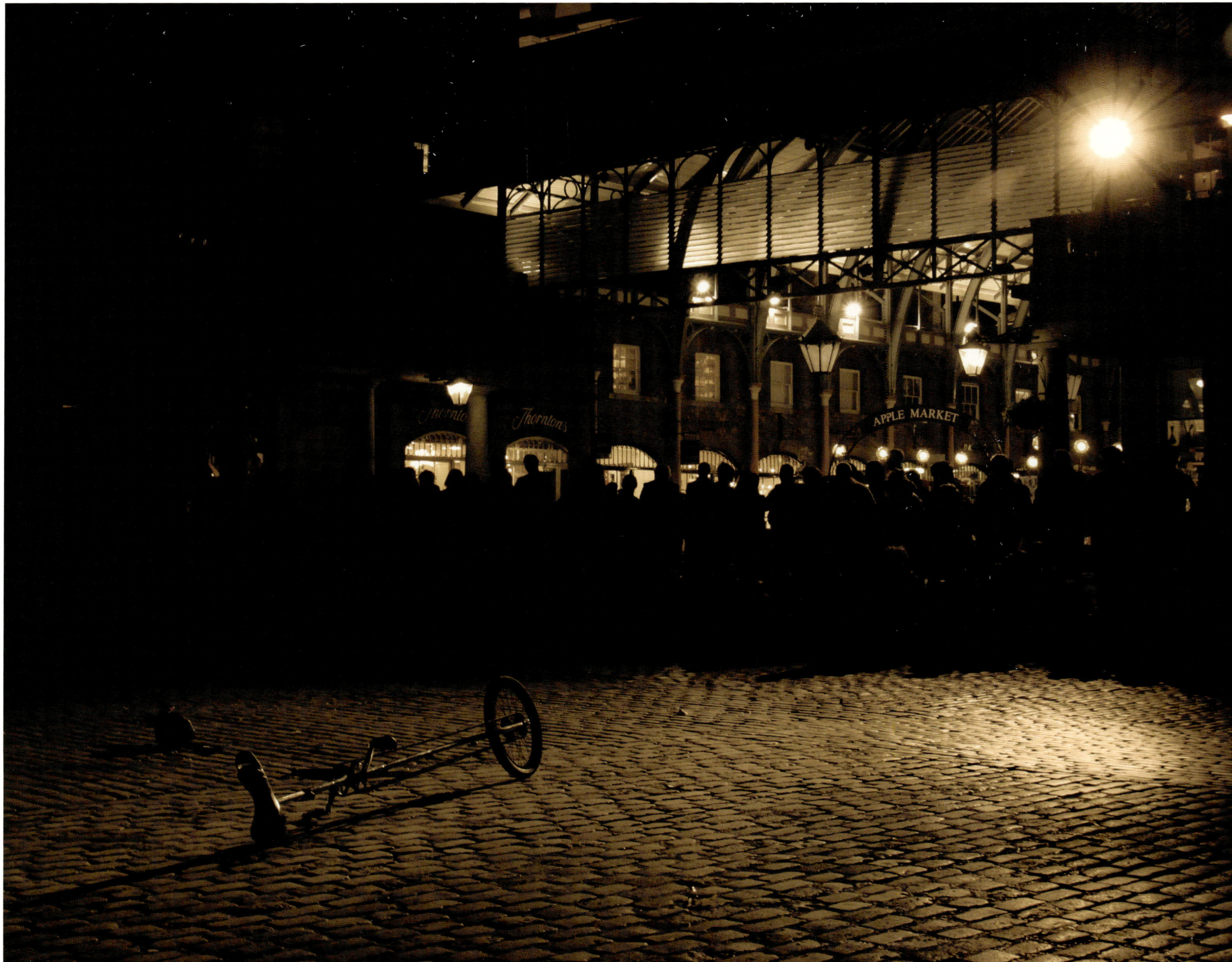
Thorntons
Thorntons
APPLE MARKET

Name: Grégoire Derudder, 26
Nationality: French
Status: Amateur
Photographer since: 2009
Favourite Camera of all Time: Rolleiflex
Influences: Willy Ronis, National Geographic publications

The Location: London, UK

The Story: I had just an evening to spend in London and went for a walk around Covent Garden. Many street performers were here. Some struggling to attract people's attention, some captivating them with unexpected performances. My attention was caught by the scene of this gathered crowd waiting feverishly for the next breathtaking act to happen. I tried to capture this mysterious atmosphere of both impatience and wonder.

The Exposure:
Camera: Canon EOS 50D
Lens: 17-50mm
Settings: F6.3 @ 1/20 sec ISO 1250
Post-production: Lightroom

Name: Guy Titley, 42
Nationality: British
Status: Amateur
Photographer since: 2006
Favourite Camera of all Time:
Canon EOS 5D
Influences: Trent Parke, Robert Cameron

The Location: Poole, UK

The Story: This fishing boat (the 'Sally-Jane') was a regular fixture in the harbour. A working fishing boat painted in bright complimentary colours, I thought it was a good subject for some pictures. I used a very wide angle lens to try and exaggerate the dimensions of the cranes, nets, and even get the quay itself into the picture. The dusk sky gives a pleasing counterpoint to the bright colours of the boat. The fishermen were happy to be photographed going about their work of mending the nets.

The Exposure:
Camera: Canon EOS 5D
Lens: Sigma 12-24 at 13mm
Settings: F5 @ 1/50 sec ISO 3200
Post-production: Photoshop

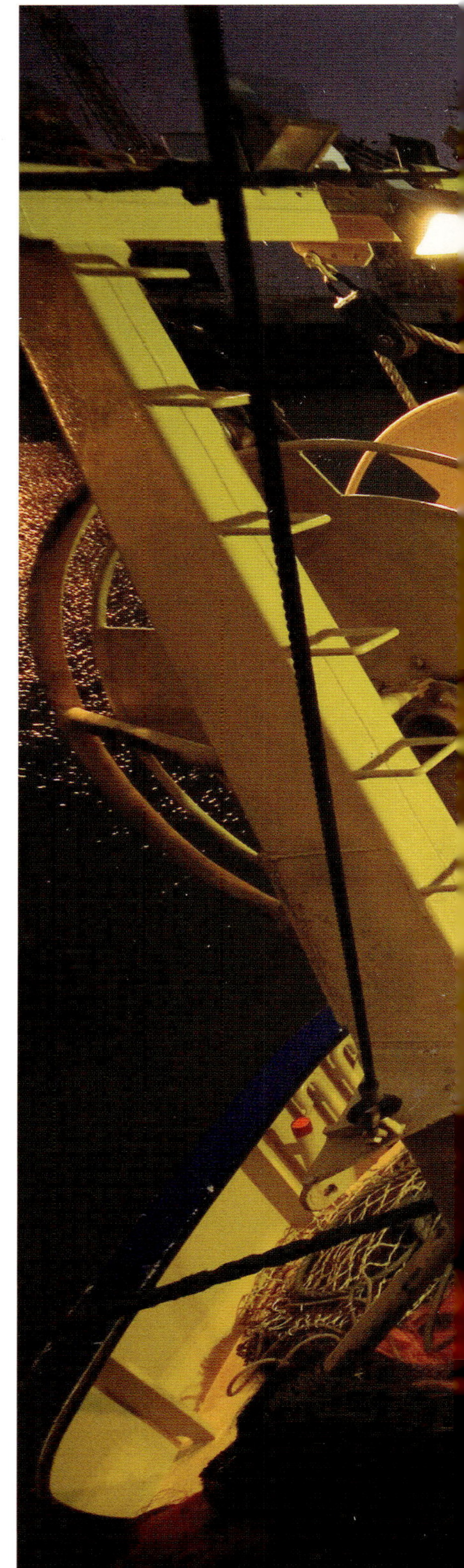

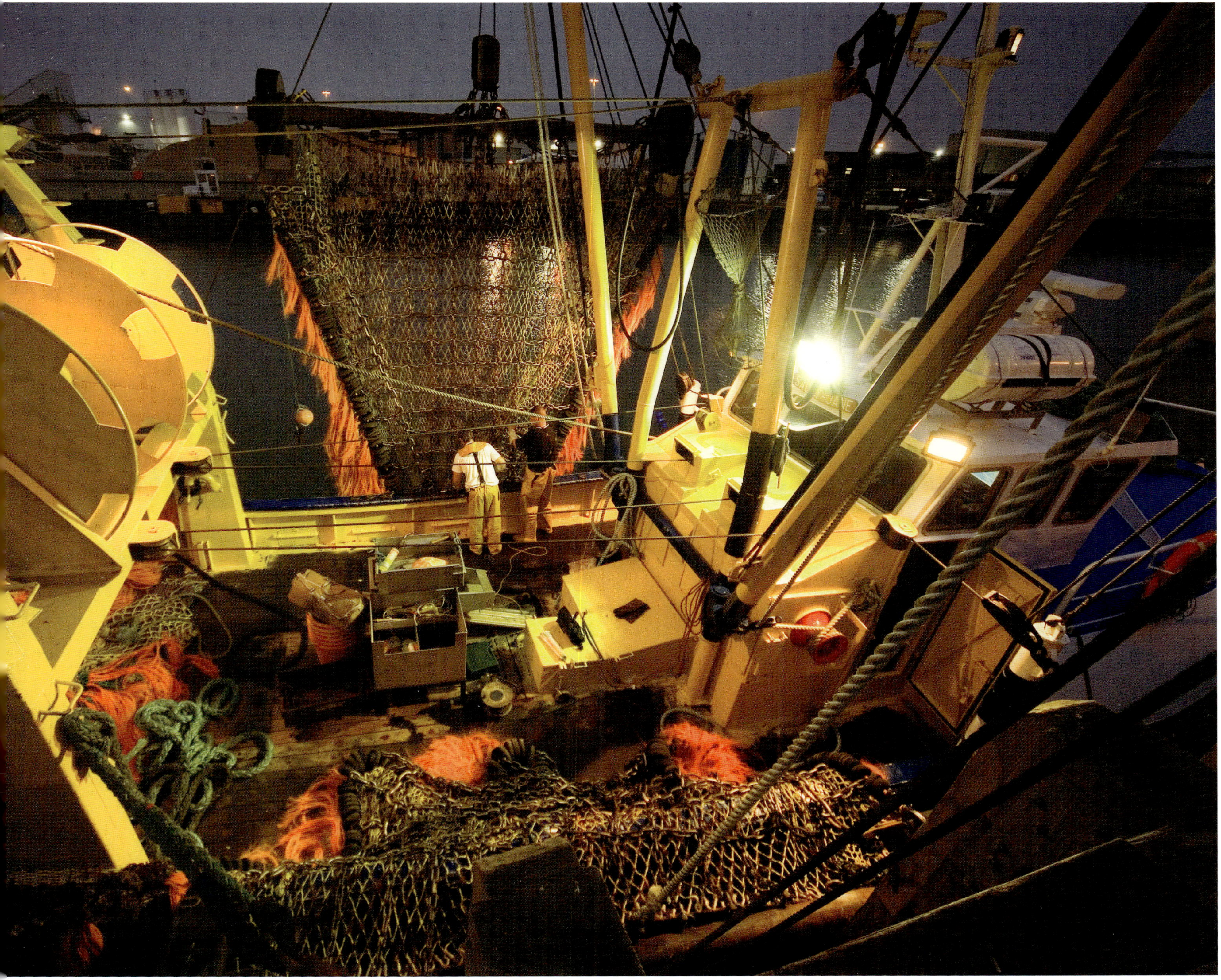

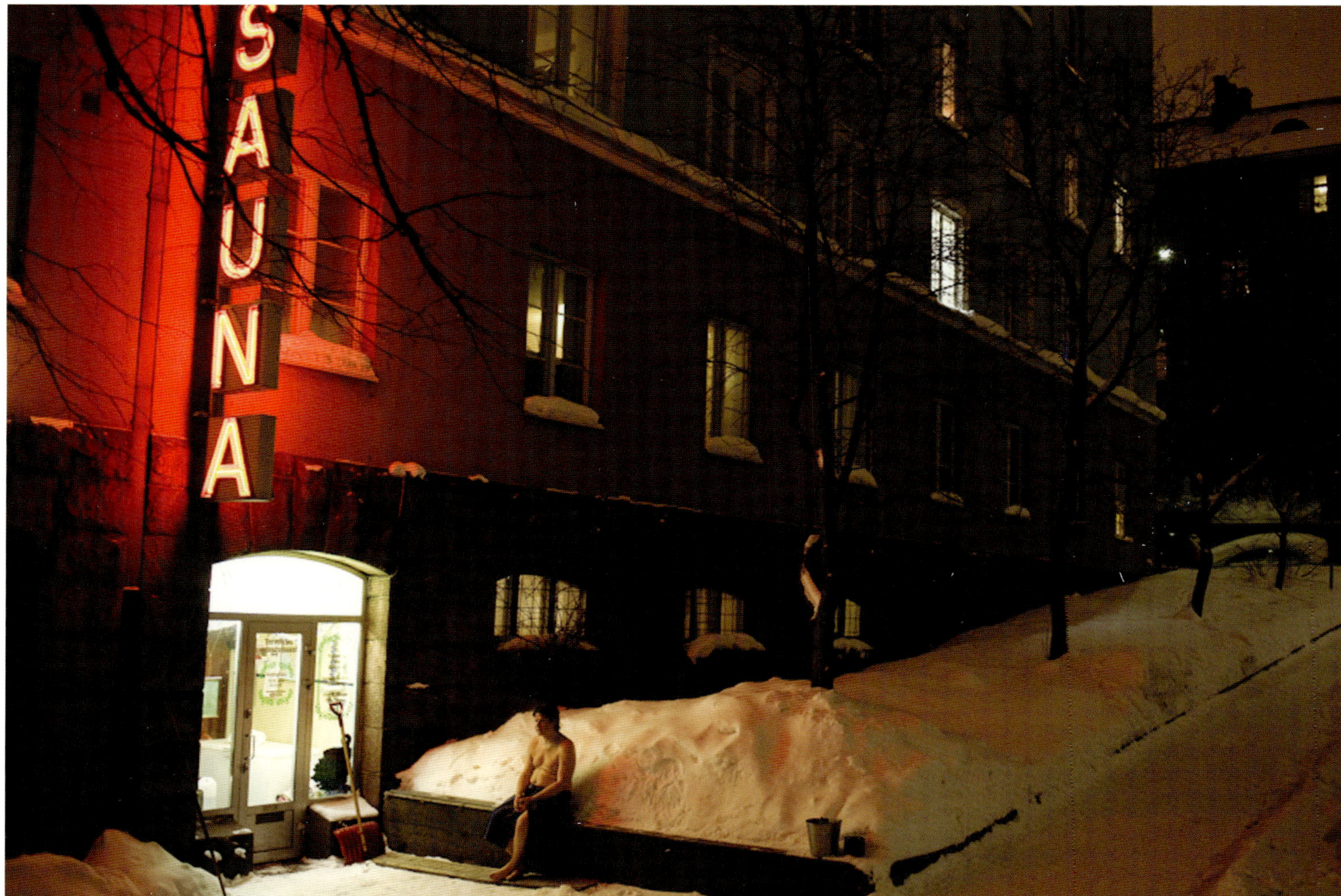
SAUNA

Name: Hugo Bes, 39
Nationality: Dutch
Status: Professional
Photographer since: 1999
Favourite Camera of all Time:
Canon EOS 5D
Influences: Henri Cartier Bresson, Ed van der Elsken

The Location: Helsinki, Finland

The Story: I had wanted to capture this scene for some time. I could never find the right angle or light until now. I had already completed a portrait series in the sauna as a free work project. When I left the sauna I noticed the guy cooling down from a sauna bath. It had been snowing for weeks in Helsinki and I climbed on a huge pile of snow that offered me the right point of view. The combination of excellent evening light and snow reflection helped me achieve the perfect shot.

The Exposure:
Camera: Canon EOS 5D
Lens: Canon 35mm F2.0
Settings: 1/30 - F2.8 ISO 800
Post-production: Contrast and lens vignetting

Name: Gabor Bagics, 31
Nationality: Hungarian
Status: Amateur
Photographer since: 2006
Favourite Camera of all Time:
Voigtlander Bessa R2A
Influences: Jeff Mermelstein, Alex Webb, Richard Kalvar

The Location: Budapest, Hungary

The Story: The 20th August is one of the biggest festivals in Hungary and it usually finishes with fireworks. I took my place before the start. I measured the time of fireworks from explosion till burn out and set the shutter speed accordingly in order to capture full "balls". The fireworks on the image exploded almost at the same time.

The Exposure:
Camera: Canon 400D
Lens: Sigma 70-300@86mm
Settings: f14, 2.5 s, ISO 200
Post-production: Photoshop

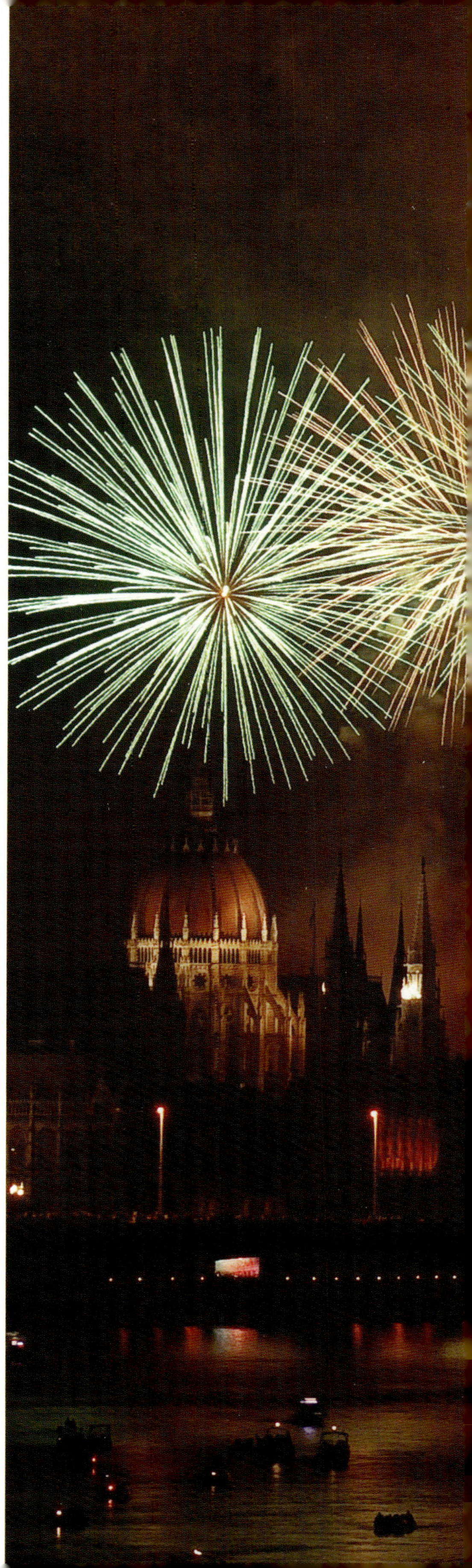

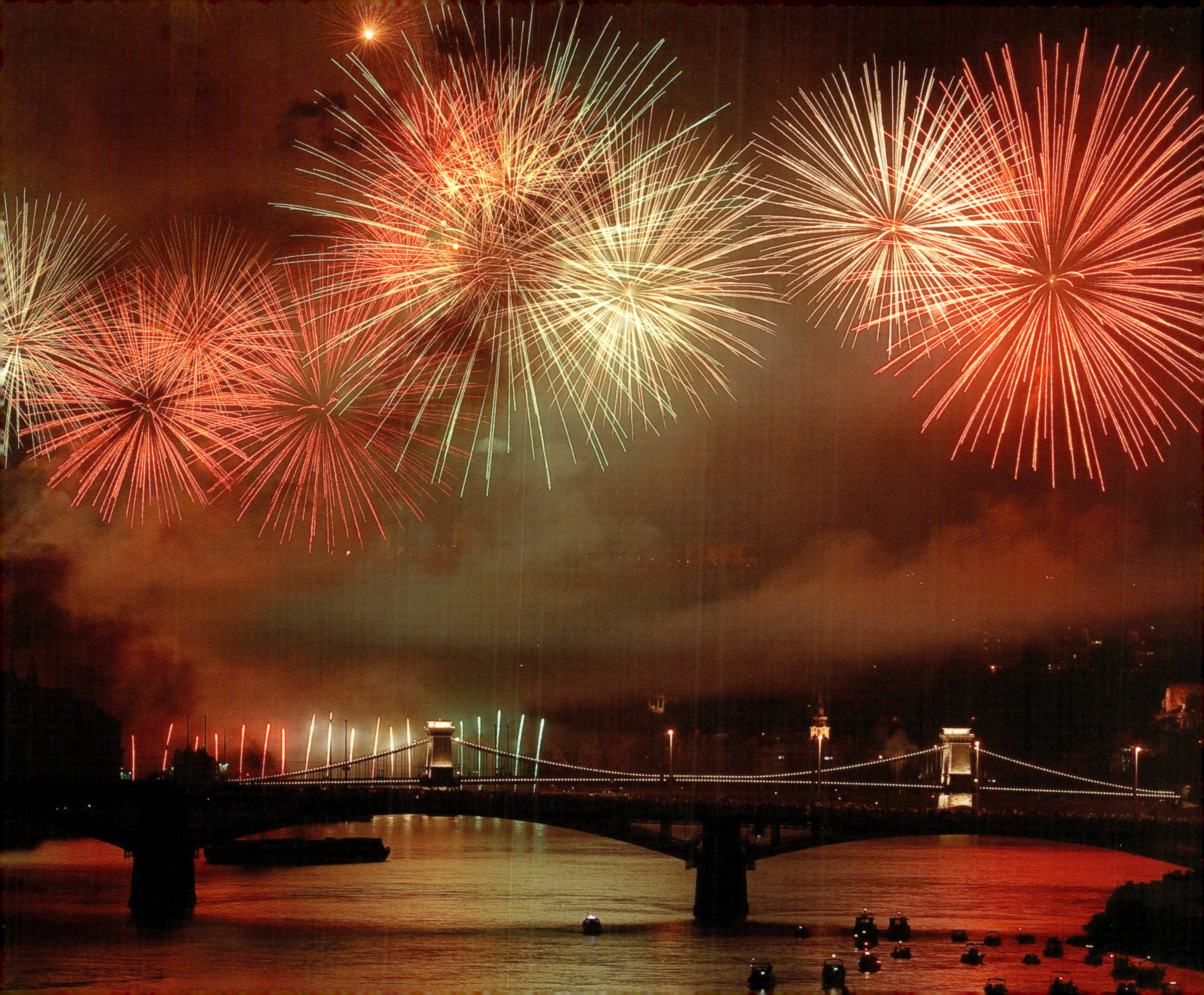

Name: Vlad Eftenie, 33
Nationality: Romanian
Status: Advanced Amateur
Photographer since: 2003
Favourite Camera of all Time: Nikon F5
Influences: The world around

The Location: Paris, France

The Story: The waiter is taking an inconspicuous break before closing time in the restaurant.

The Exposure:
Camera: Nikon F5
Lens: F2.8
Settings: F2.8 @ 1/25 sec ISO 400
Post-production: 35mm scan with Nikon ED V, no editing

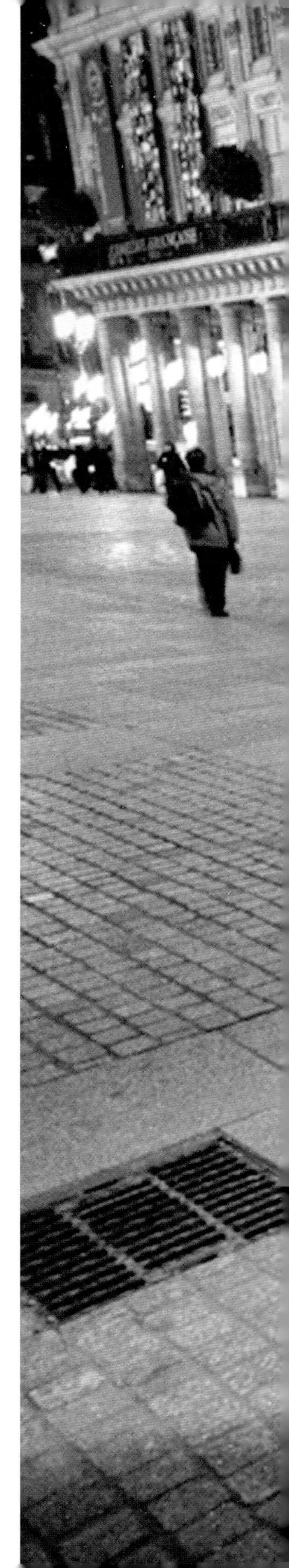

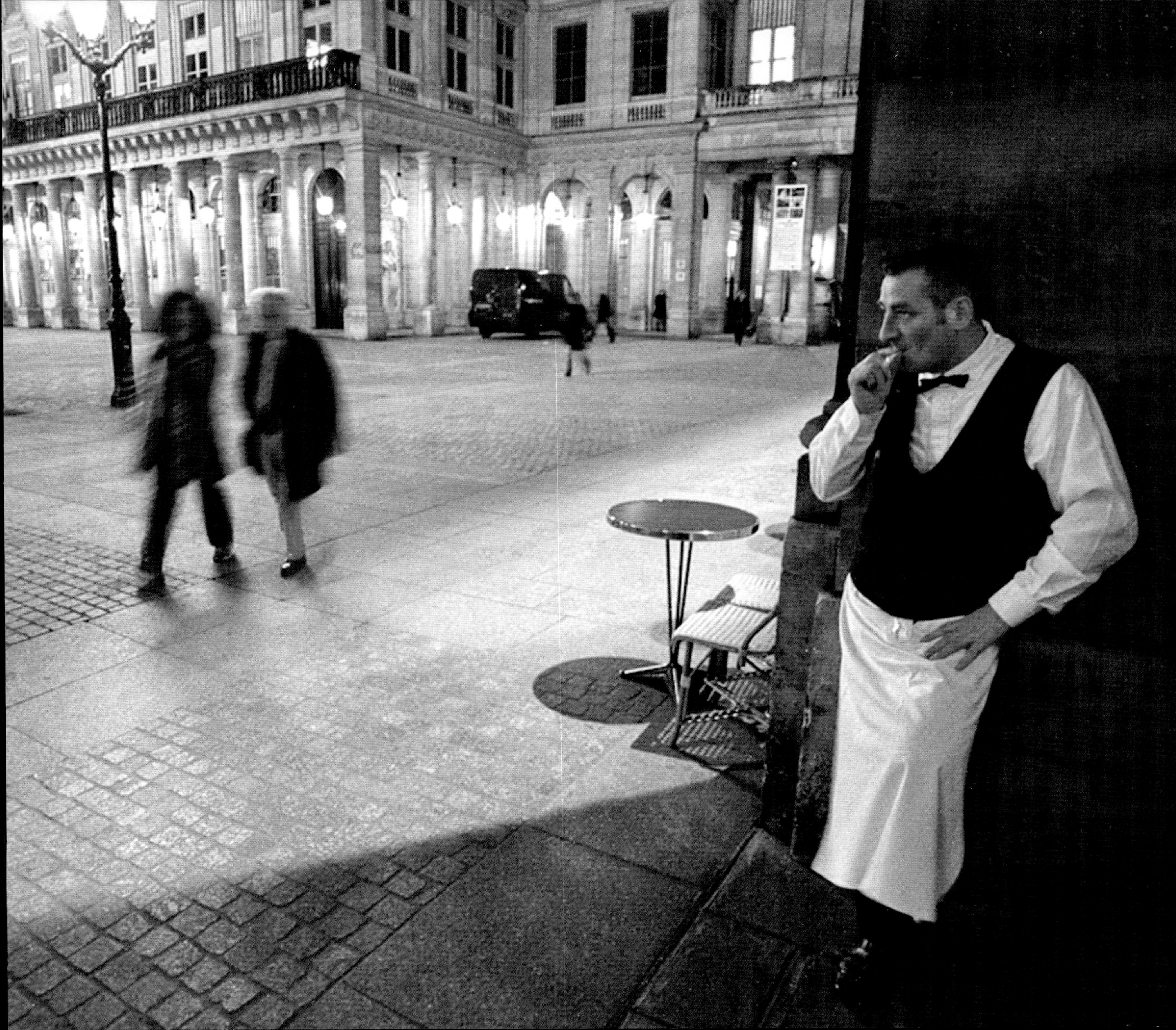

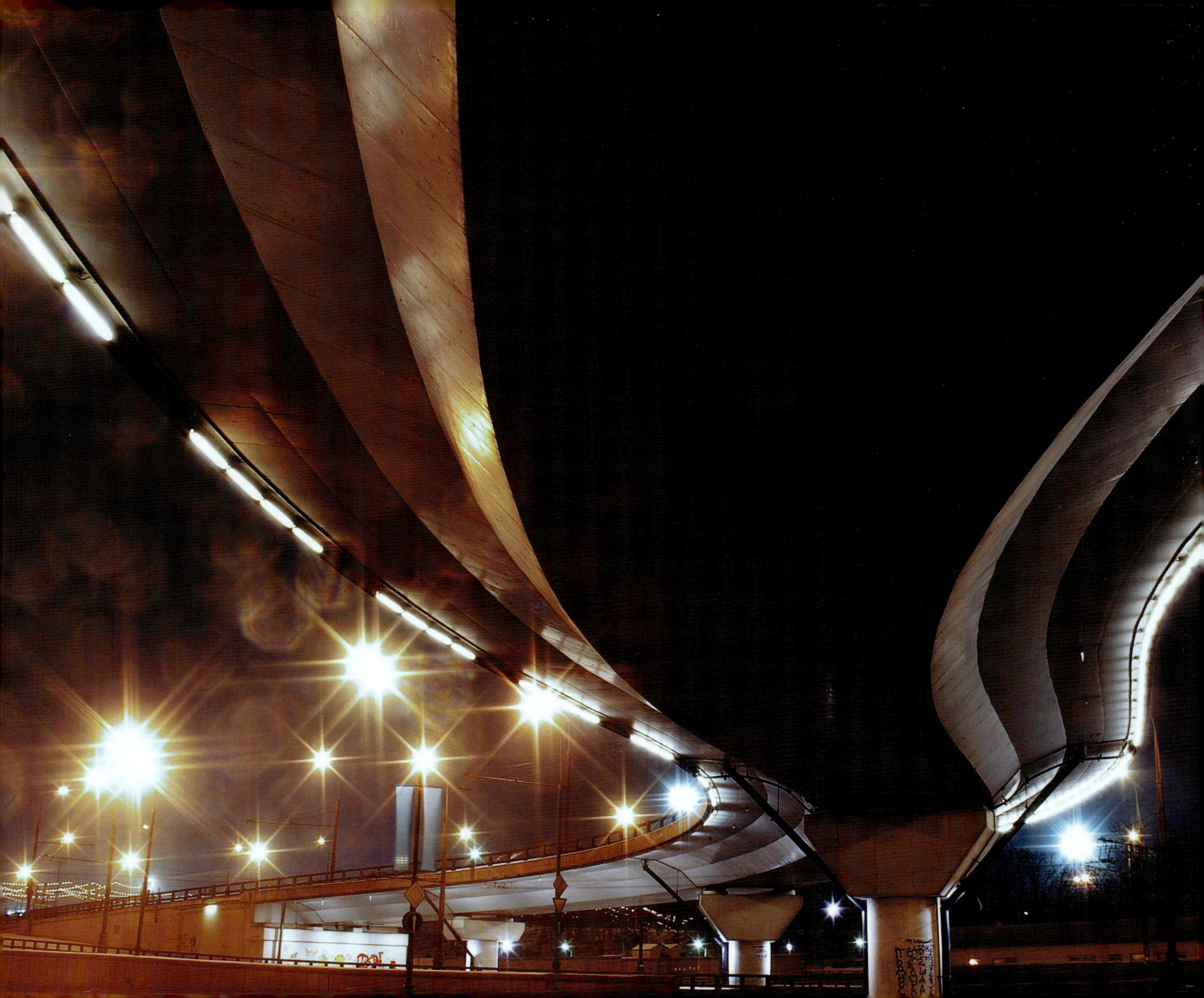

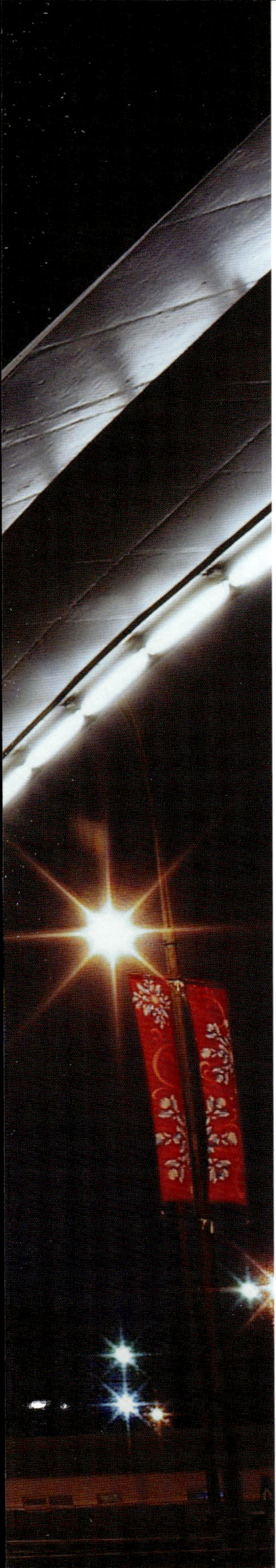

Name: Pavel Roshkov, 43
Nationality: Russian
Status: Amateur
Photographer since: 1982
Favourite Camera of all Time: Pentax *ist DS
Influences: Ansel Adams, Michael Kenna

The Location: Moscow, Russia

The Story: This is the view that the thousands who drive over this everyday do not see. From this angle the road is almost like a starship or the Milky Way across the sky. A real example of the hidden beauty of architecture and how pure forms have a very natural feel to them.

The Exposure:
Camera: Pentax *ist DS
Lens: Pentax SMC FA 24 mm F2 AL(IF)
Settings: 24mm, F11 ISO 100
Post-production: Photoshop levels in CS3

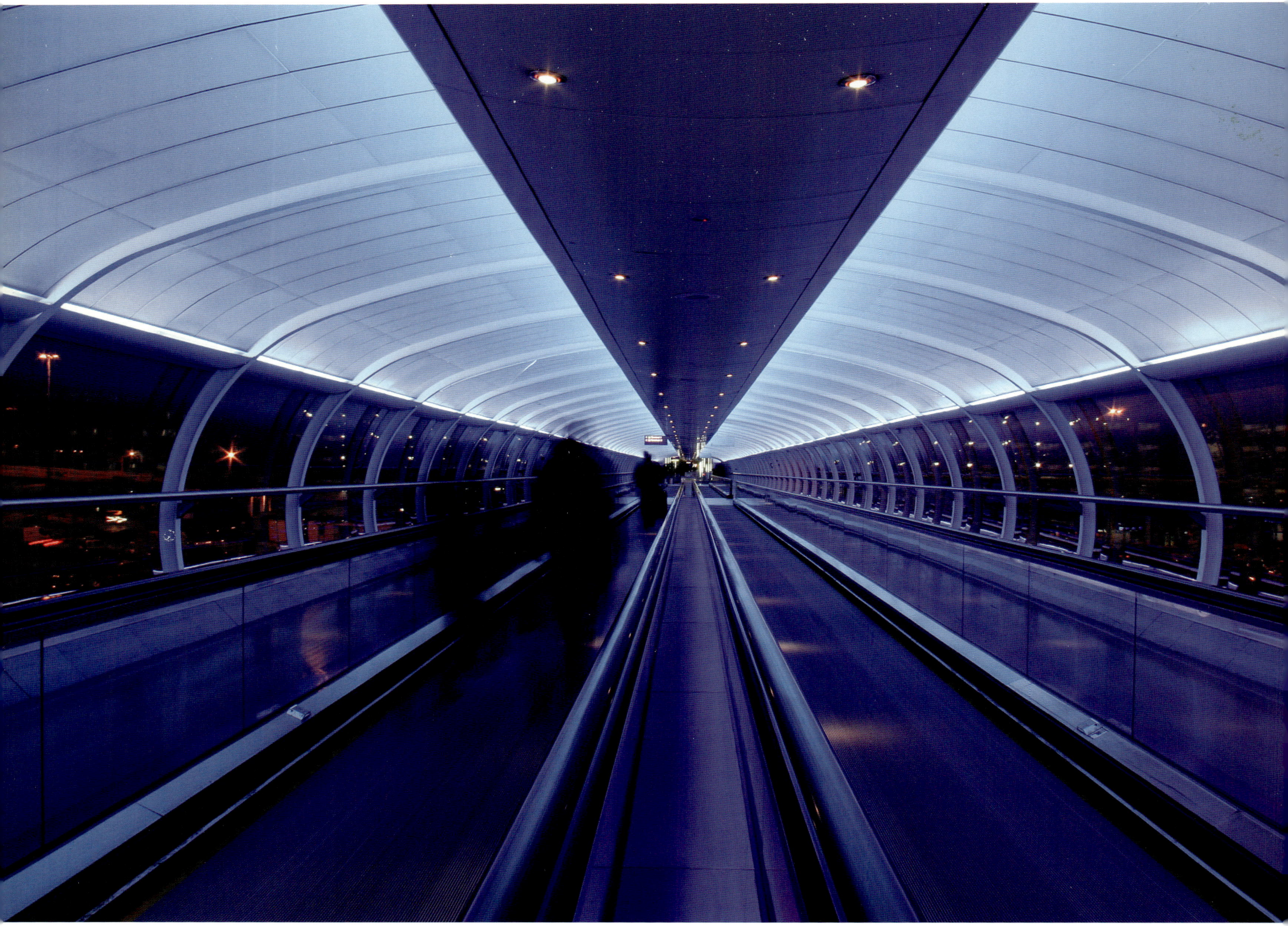

Name: Diane Seddon, 53
Nationality: British
Status: Professional
Photographer since: 2005
Favourite Camera of all Time:
Canon 1D Mark IV
Influences: Henri Cartier Bresson

The Location: Manchester, UK

The Story: I was exploring the airport and saw the long corridor which links the air terminal with the railway station. All the blues, together with the outside lights just seemed to come together. The image was taken on a tripod using the centre of the walkway for support. I expected airport security to ask me what I was doing, or tell me I shouldn't be there. No one came, and I was able to get a series of images, of which this was my favourite.

The Exposure:
Camera: Canon 350D
Lens: 17-85 4.5 - 5.6 @ 17mm
Settings: F19, 1.5 seconds, ISO 200
Post-production: Photoshop

Name: Tom Scott, 30
Nationality: British
Status: Semi-Professional
Photographer since: 2006
Favourite Camera of all Time:
Hasselblad H4D 31
Influences: Mary Kelly, Martin Parr,
David Lachapelle

The Location: Dublin, Ireland

The Story: I stood on tip-toes at the rear of the venue hoping to capture the poetic atmosphere during the Bell X1 gig. I had to dodge the bobbing heads in the foreground, fortunately it all worked out.

The Exposure:
Camera: Olympus E-3
Lens: F2.0 50mm Macro
Settings: F2.0 1/40 ISO 800
Post-production: Aperture 3 –
desaturate and contrast

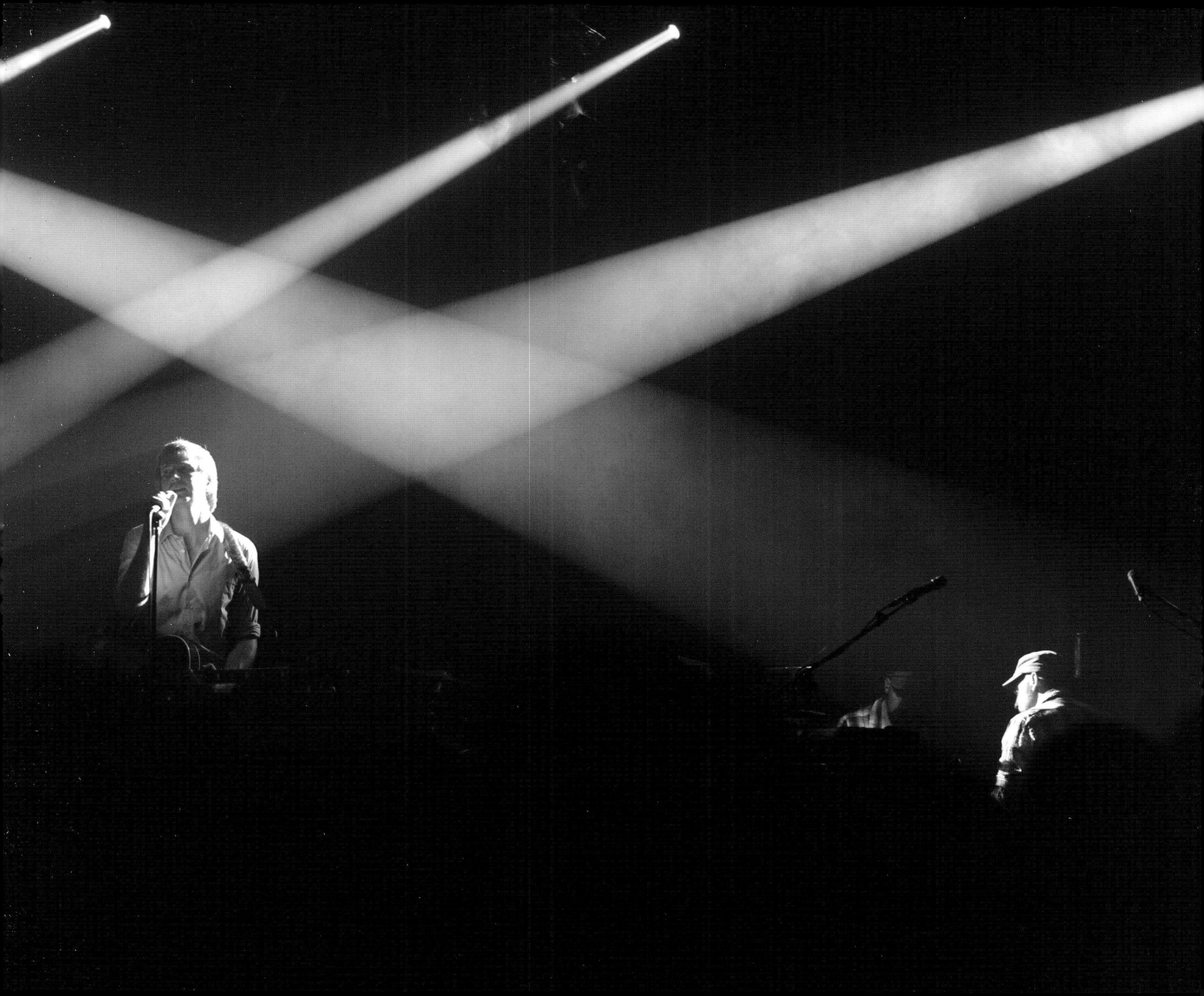

Name: Mark Wilkinson, 44
Nationality: Scottish
Status: Documentary Photographer
Photographer since: 2000
Favourite Camera of all Time: Lieca M6
Influences: Robert Frank, Walker Evans, Diane Arbus

The Location: London, UK

The Story: This is a of a busker underneath Waterloo Bridge on the South Bank of London. It was a spontaneous moment and there was only just enough light for the shot to come out at a slow shutter speed.

The Exposure:
Camera: Yashicaflex Twin Lens
Settings: F3.5 @ 1/20th second ISO 1600
Post-production: Photoshop

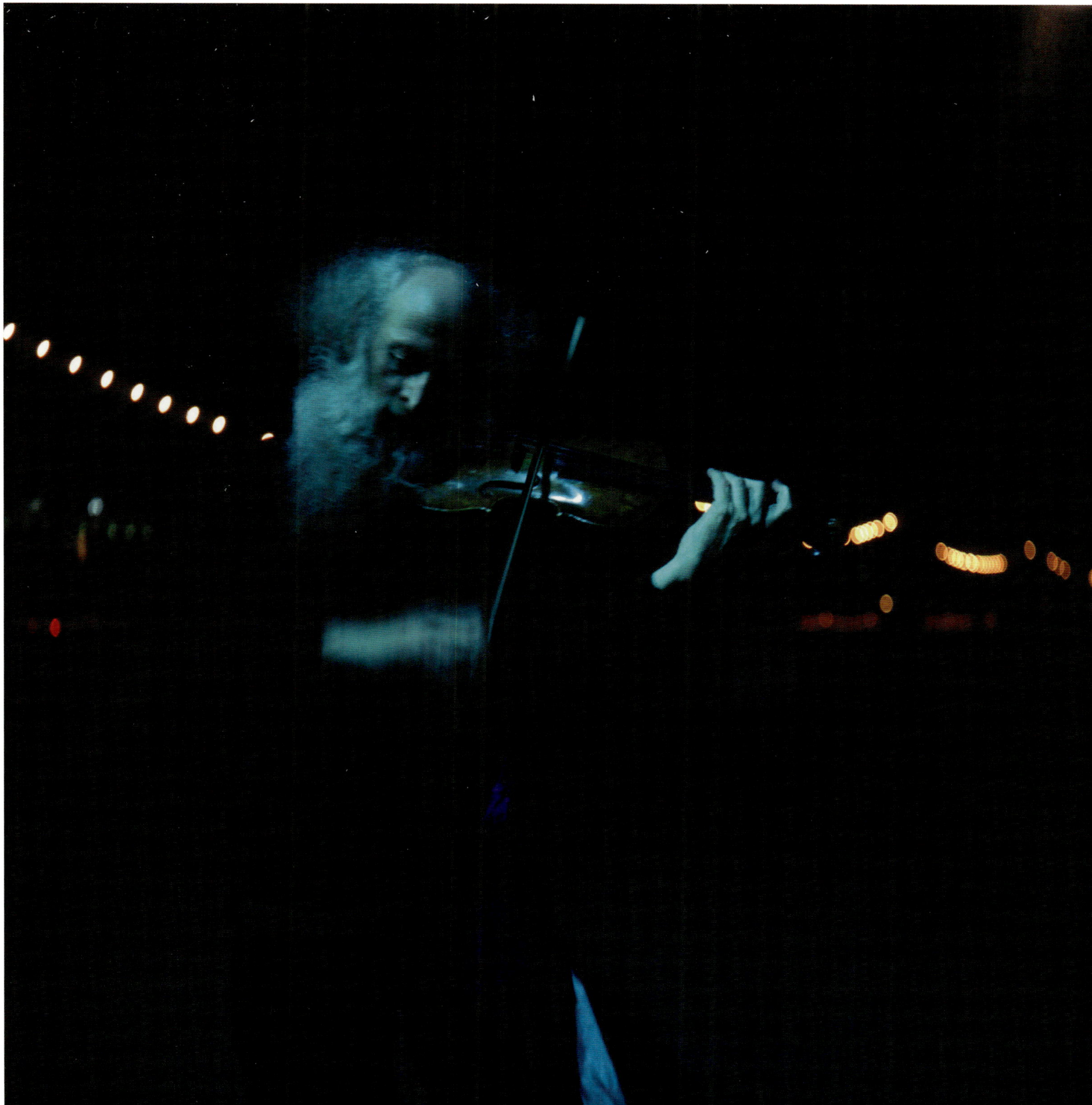

Acknowledgement
Our sponsors

This competition requires a great deal of commitment from a lot of people to make it work. But without great prizes you have little incentive to enter. So we are extremely proud of our sponsors and their contribution to the competition. They are more than partners, they inspire and motivate us all with their generosity and involvement. We would like to thank them all very much for their participation and making the competition so strong and so exciting.

Billingham

YERBURY
EXCELLENCE THROUGH PASSION
MENTORING SEMINARS WORKSHOPS TRAINING

akm music

onOne Software

PLASTIC SANDWICH
Leather Print Books

radiopopper

PHOTODEX CORPORATION

Perma Jet

NATIONAL GEOGRAPHIC™

SIM2000 IMAGING.COM

VisibleDust

Nik® Software

SWPP & BPPA QUALIFIED member

theimagefile...

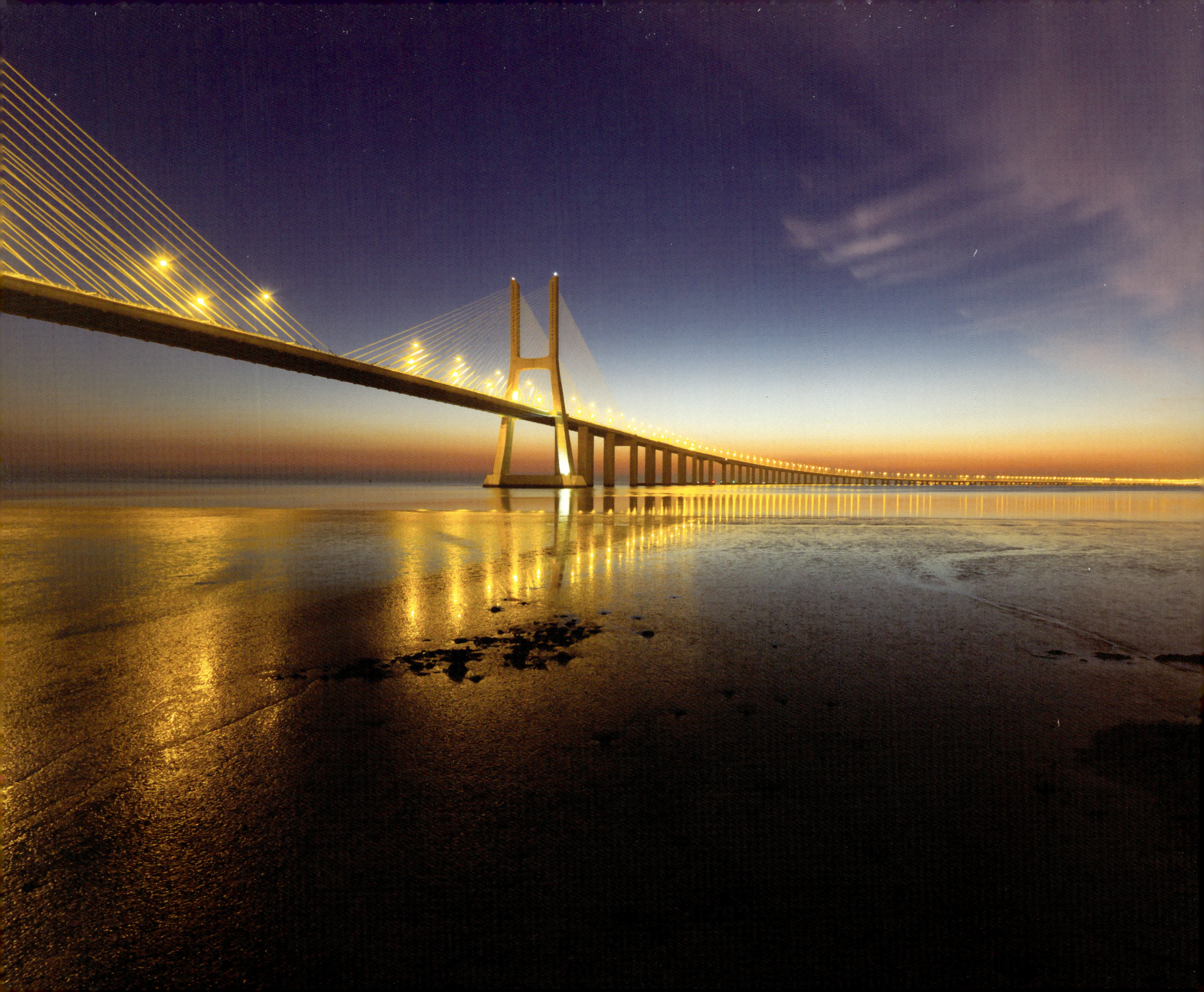

MIX
Paper from responsible sources
FSC® C016446

Printed on Revive 50% recycled paper using vegetable inks.